CRUISING UNDER POWER

CRUISING UNDER POWER

AN INSIDER'S GUIDE TO THE PLEASURES OF POWERBOAT CRUISING

KATY BURKE

1661

ILLUSTRATIONS BY

TAZ WALLER

G. P. PUTNAM'S SONS

New York

G. P. Putnam's Sons
Publishers Since 1838
200 Madison Avenue
New York, NY 10016

Library of Congress Cataloging-in-Publication Data

Burke, Katy.
Cruising under power : an insider's guide to the pleasures of
powerboat cruising / Katy Burke; illustrations by Taz Waller.
      p.   cm.
1. Motorboats.   2. Boats and boating.   I. Title.
GV835.B78   1991   90-32690   CIP
                       797.1'25—dc20

ISBN 0-399-13515-4

Printed in the United States of America

1 2 3 4 5 6 7 8 9 10

This book is printed on acid-free paper.
∞

For Taz—best friend, lover, husband, shipmate,
and builder of our beautiful motor yacht, Duchess

Acknowledgments

A BOOK OF THIS TYPE is never written alone. Without the help and support of literally hundreds of people, it never would have happened. The biggest thanks, as always, goes to fellow cruisers who were willing to spend hours sharing their experiences and their ideas about cruising in a powerboat, as well as allowing me to poke through their home-away-from-home. I'm lucky to live in Oriental, which is a favorite stop of the "snowbirds" traveling south or north according to the seasons. I checked the town docks and the marinas almost daily to see who was in and what kind of boat they had. I was impressed by both the number of cruising powerboats and the kindness and generosity of their owners. Besides gathering lots of material, we made a lot of new friends in the process.

While I can't begin to name them all, special thanks must go to John Sheffield and Kathleen Jennings, who wrote long informative letters while cruising in the Bahamas, and who also brought their Krogen 54, *Dolphin Dancer,* up my narrow little creek, proving once and for all the value of a bow thruster; to Reaney and Mary McGilvray aboard their wonderful old wooden cruiser, *Dolphin*; to Rose and Dudley Boycott aboard their Marine Trader, *Myth*; to Ed and Wanda Lange aboard their lovely Grand Banks, *Wandalust*; to Clarence and Joan Hyde, who let me spend hours crawling through their beautifully maintained Krogen 42, *Joan M*; to Fred and Anne Kist, professional captain and crew of the impeccable Consolidated Commuter, *Ragtime*; to Joel and Christine Mele of the Viking, *Christine Marie*; and to Jill Lorenz, who took numerous photographs while cruising with the Meles; to Karen and Richard Brashear for sharing their great memories of cruising and living aboard their classic motor yacht, *Tyee*, in Washington and the San Juans; and to Candace Young and Norm Czuchra, sailors-turned-powerboaters and the best charter boat partners we've ever had.

Doug Gaither and Bert Quay read portions of the manuscript and offered valuable suggestions and criticisms, in addition to the excellent help given by my editor at Putnam, Betsy Perry.

A great deal of expert information and photographs were provided by manufacturers of both boats and marine equipment. Thanks go to Julie Richardson at Hatteras, Jim Krogen at Kadey-Krogen Yachts, Al Hill and Jerry Husted at Nordic Tugs, Jerry Warren of Jefferson Yachts, Sally Forker of Caterpillar Engines, Don Harrington of Fireboy Systems, Jim Blaney at Aquadrive Systems, Dominique Dart of Soundown Corporation, John Scippa at General Ecology, Don Forster at Sea Recovery, R. J. Smith of Galley Maid, G. James Lippmann at American Boat and Yacht Council, Lynn Dougan of Marinco, Bob Summers of Trace Engineering, John Surrette of Rolls Battery Engineering, Don Welles at Surrette America, William O'Brien of Raritan, Stephen Goldman at Lightning Electronics, Jeanette Ogilvie of Atkins & Hoyle, D. L. Menichella at Daimen Corporation, Fred McKaig of Mooring Products, Eric Braitmayer of Imtra, Jan Lockie of Basic Designs, Will Keene at The Edson Corporation, Norm Wright at Nicro Marine, Sue and Wally Chappin at Oriental Sailmakers, Emily Koepp at Venture Marine, Diane Cox at Nautical Engineering, Kathy Gartner at Peugeot, Ronald Means of Shakespeare, John Jonny of Minolta, Peter Rachtman and Jerry Truax at So-Pac, Elizabeth Harris at Down East Sails and Canvas, Bill Clark at Standard Communications, Ron Day at Micrologic, Mary Kay Schlaefer of Raytheon, Armand Bouchard of Alden Electronics, Bob Selig, Jr. at Davis Instruments, William Kuenzel at ACR Electronics, and Ardith Bonnar at Survival Technologies Group.

And last but by no means least, a big thank-you to my husband, Taz, for his illustrations, his "first-line" proofreading, his thoughts and suggestions, but mostly for his love and support through it all.

Contents

Stoves, CNG Stoves, Microwaves, Barbecue Grills—
Refrigeration—Stowage—Garbage

Preface

As a marine surveyor, I have advised hundreds of purchase decisions over the past decade. In the course of nearly every survey, the buyer asks some form of the question, "Is this the right boat for me?" Their legitimate concern is voiced in a variety of ways like: "Is this a good boat? Is this a good deal? Will it go to the islands? Is it fast enough? Is it comfortable? Is the resale good on these boats?"

My job as surveyor and consultant is not to make the buying decision for the buyers by proxy but to lay out the choices for them by addressing the likely consequences of the design, features, and condition of the boat. That task is similar to what Katy is doing in this book for crews who are interested in power-yacht cruising.

I offer two caveats in your search for a satisfactory (not proper, perfect, or ultimate) cruising boat. First, understand the priorities, compromises, and unresolved conflicts inherent in the cruising lifestyle that best suits your crew before you get down to the specifics of boat and gear.

People universally demand too much of their boat when they can't form a clear picture of how they are going to use it. The old cliché that "every boat's a compromise" is probably the most intelligent-sounding but empty phrase that gets tossed around by waterfront pundits in order to justify any old tub. But a boat that has been made into "all things for all people" soon goes on the market because it disappoints the whole crew.

A friend recently made the transition from sail to power. His old sailboat had turned out to be totally unsatisfactory. He had chosen the centerboard version because his wife was afraid of running aground. And he installed roller furling because he hated to change jibs. Then he added spinnaker gear so his son could race it. But it wouldn't go to weather because of the shoal draft, it still ran aground when he strayed outside the channel, and the genoa was never right for the wind speed. So it was a bad boat.

The new power yacht is a nice convertible sportsfisherman. It has an icemaker, generator, microwave, extra water, custom furniture, and two air conditioners for his wife's comfort. It has outriggers, a fighting chair, and a rocket launcher on the half-tower so his son can chase billfish. It has full electronics in the enclosed bridge for him to play with. And it stays tied to the dock because his wife still prefers the condo, the son can't get to the fishing grounds in time with all the extra weight and windage that knocks a 22-knot boat back 16, and my friend is completely intimidated by trying to handle an expensive, twin-screw boat. He complained to the dealer that the boat just doesn't meet his expectations.

The lesson has been lost on him twice, and the boats are still taking the blame. Of course, the problem is seldom with the boat, but generally with an owner's inability to prioritize his cruising goals or to sort out the consequences of the conflicting demands he places on the boat. Too frequently, the hard drivers who are used to always having their way with people think they can have everything in a boat, too, simply by being insistent.

The other caveat is that cruising pleasure is much more the result of a happy attitude and good seamanship than of a boat perfected with all the right equipment.

Every boat is a reflection of the owner's personality. The vanity of ownership is heady, especially when the boat is expensively customized to meet your personal desires. It's a seductive game, this equipping of the boat to reflect the "wisdom" of your experience and knowledge. And buying all sorts of wonderful presents for the stock boat is a fun way of making it yours, of taking possession of the impersonal object.

Some owners, who are rightfully unsure of their seamanship abilities, try to vaccinate themselves against disaster by bolting on more equipment. They would be better served by investing their time in exercising those skills than in pouring through the gear catalogues for another nautical amulet.

Still, the pride of ownership pales when the boat merely sits in port. Boats are beautiful all polished up at the marina, but that's not what cruising boats are for.

Katy Burke has never been one to just "lay to the dock." Over the past couple of decades, she has spent nearly half her time cruising, and the other half getting ready for the next voyage. Treat her as your consultant on cruising in powerboats. She strikes a practical balance between necessary seamanship and good equipment. And most importantly, she explains why particular configurations and gear work best in the circumstances you're likely to encounter afloat.

The value of this book lies not only in the concreteness of her own experience but also in the questions that lead you to a clearer understanding of the demands of your own cruising style.

The real enjoyment of cruising lies in the doing rather than the owning. It's not how the boat handles, but how you handle the boat, that gives genuine pleasure. It's not how your boat looks, but how you look at the boat, that satisfies your soul. It's not owning, but using the boat well, that creates the good memories.

The boat should not be the object of a possessive perfectionism that controls us or sucks the fun and color out of our precious cruising time. Instead, it ought to be an instrument of our laughter and joy, a vehicle that responds to the playfulness in our souls. It ought to be a toy that we use, even use up, in free play.

Go now and have fun.

Bert Quay, Marine Surveyor
Editor, *The Harbor Guide*
Oriental, N.C.
Fall 1989

Introduction

A LOT OF PEOPLE still think of me as a sailor; or more often now, as a former sailor-turned-powerboater. In fact, my first boat was a powerboat—a 24-foot Owens cabin cruiser, and I put an awful lot of cruising miles on her. There is nothing remarkable about this, except that at the time I didn't have the slightest idea what I was doing. But I did it anyway, survived, and learned plenty in the process.

Then I discovered the "romance" of sail, and became a full-time live-aboard and cruising sailor. I think much of the romance of it had to do with youth, because in looking back I can see a lot of hard work and a lot of "camping out" and a lot of struggling to make ends meet so we could keep cruising. Not that I regret it; I don't. I wouldn't have missed any of those experiences for the world.

But as we get older I think we get a little more practical. Taz and I finally admitted out loud what we had secretly known for a long time—that we spent the majority of our time under power, and were paying a hefty price, in terms of space, comfort and maintenance, just to carry all that "romance" aloft, which, in fact, was seldom used.

Our search for a cruising powerboat led us by chance to the offices

of Jay Benford, who is a dear friend as well as a fellow naval architect. We had no intention of building a boat from scratch, but Taz
spotted some drawings on Jay's board for a Solarium 44 and that was
the end of the search. *Duchess* was conceived, and the work, and
headaches, and joy, began. At times I thought we were truly nuts,
but I have to say that I love *Duchess* more than any other boat I have
ever owned. Although there are now others who think we are truly
nuts (all that varnish to keep up!), she is, for us, perfect.

It has pleased me to discover that sailors and powerboaters alike
respond to her, and to us the owners, in such a positive way. I don't
think it is just *Duchess*, but that the cruising community as a whole
has become less polarized. Where there was once a sailing community and a power community, there is now a *cruising* community,
made up of people who simply like to cruise, never mind what kind
of boat they happen to own. Part of this may be due to the fact that
sailors in ever-increasing numbers are discovering the pleasures of
powerboating (we've stopped borrowing ice cubes and gotten ice-
makers of our own).

When Taz and I made the switch from sail to power, I was more
than a little nervous about telling some of our dyed-in-the-wool
sailing friends about our decision. To my surprise, many of them
confided that they either had their sailboat up for sale or were
seriously (or secretly) thinking about getting into power.

All the reasons why is not what this book is about. Suffice it to say
that more and more people are cruising under power these days, and
as a result our attitudes are changing and our boats are changing.
Since cruising implies covering long distances, we want a boat that
will take us places in comfort and safety, and do it economically as
well. As we travel to more out-of-the-way places, and spend more
time at anchor, we want a boat that gives us a greater measure of
independence from the shore.

Boat owners are making changes to their boats (I don't know a
single boat owner who *isn't* constantly tinkering with something or
another)—adding equipment, rearranging or adding storage space,
improving ventilation, figuring out where to stash the snorkeling
gear—all with an eye toward making it a better boat for cruising.
And manufacturers are responding to the increased interest in cruising, both in the kinds of boats they are building and in the type of
gear they are installing.

In the following chapters, we'll explore why some boats are better for cruising than others, and look at ways to improve the boat we already own. The more we can do to make our boat more comfortable, more seaworthy, and easier to handle, the more fun it will be; and that is, after all, why we go cruising in the first place.

But let's not lose sight of the most important facet of cruising. It is simply the act of getting on your boat, and *going*. The rest of this book will be full of suggestions and recommendations, and hopefully you will find some ideas of value, but they are still just that: suggestions and recommendations. The boat must be sound and a certain amount of equipment is necessary, of course, but I have seen too many people get so involved in searching for the perfect boat, or in "getting ready," that they never seem to go. And that's too bad, because I know what they're missing.

When we have dropped anchor in a tranquil cove at the end of a passage, when we put up our feet and lean back on the cushions to watch the sunset together, as we discuss the day's events and look forward to exploring ashore the next day, we feel at peace with our world and with each other and we know why we're there. And it does not matter one whit whether or not we got there using new, improved, color radar, or a new, improved loran with two extra waypoints, or just a compass. It only matters that we got there.

Cruising is pure joy. It's not for everybody, and I'm glad of that, or our waterways would be as crowded as a freeway at rush hour. It brings different joys to different people, and it certainly brings its own set of challenges. We learn to take the bad with the good, and overcoming difficulties makes us feel good about ourselves.

Not long ago, someone told me they went cruising to escape the constant stress imposed by their job, and they found that cruising was full of stress too, but somehow it was "different." I suspect the difference is this: when we're cruising, the problems are immediate, and we deal with them immediately. Coming around a bend and meeting a tug and barge head-on may be stressful, dragging anchor may be stressful, but we deal with these things at once and the stress is gone. Job-related stress, or the stress of coping with life in a crowded city, can be the kind of stress we carry around constantly like some kind of excess baggage, and that's the stuff that's harmful. I've never known anyone who has gotten sick because they went cruising. I have known a lot of people who have become healthier because they went cruising. It's a fine way of life, and once the cruising bug bites, the rash doesn't go away until you do. But don't take my word for it, go find out for yourself. Meanwhile, let's get on with my suggestions and recommendations, because I do have a few to share.

Katy Burke, aboard *Duchess*
Oriental, N.C.
August 1989

CRUISING UNDER POWER

CHAPTER 1

Boats for Cruising

WHILE IT'S TRUE that just about any boat can be used for cruising, and I've certainly seen people cruising in every conceivable kind of boat, there are still differences that make some boats more suitable than others. Some of us may be happy with small and simple, and for others only large and luxurious will do, but there are certain basics that I think we all insist on—full standing headroom (you may not find this in every cabin in some older boats), bunks that are wide enough and long enough for comfortable sleeping (you may not find this on some newer boats), a workable galley, a roomy head with a shower, an engine room that's easily accessible, a deck area that affords comfortable sitting and lounging. I could go on and on with generalities, but we all know it's the specifics that make the difference. Only you can decide what specifics you must have and what compromises you are willing to make, and I've never seen a boat purchase yet that didn't include some compromises.

Yet, even though some compromise will be inevitable, there are so many styles available today that you can literally pick and choose. Most production boats are semi-displacement cruisers, usually with a fly bridge, but you'll also find marvelous tug "yachts," hefty trawlers, yachts designed after lobster or fishing boats, even small freighters capable of carrying a jeep as deck cargo. In the used-boat market, the choices are even greater.

SIZE

Powerboats come in all sizes, but the trend seems to be toward larger boats every year (Figure 1-1). I know of at least one major manufacturer who is tooling-up to add a "stock" 90-footer to their line. I remember when anything under 30 feet was considered "small." Now it's anything under 40 feet. We can speculate on any number of reasons why this is so. Perhaps it's that we're simply becoming a more affluent society, and the natural tendency is to buy as much or as big as we can afford. Certainly there is a tendency to trade up to a larger boat as we become proficient with our present one, and manufacturers naturally respond to this "trade-up factor." Or that same affluence that allows us more "goodies" at home carries over into our boats. We want more and more goodies afloat, too, and that means a bigger boat to hold them all.

Age probably has something to do with it, too. Are cruising folks, as a group, getting older? Could be. People are retiring younger, and no longer content to spend their "golden years" in a rocking chair on the front porch, watching the world go by. They are still very much *with* the world, and with a retirement income, and—finally—the time to relax and do for weeks or months on end what they used to do on weekends: go cruising. But after fifty years or so of "the good life" they aren't necessarily ready to trade in the comforts of home for a spartan existence on a small boat; hence, the trend toward bigger boats.

One of the most important factors to consider when determining what size boat you need, or want, is a realistic appraisal of how you will use her. It's hard to justify the expense of a 50-foot passage-making trawler if your cruising will be limited to perhaps one month out of the year and within a few-hundred-miles' radius of your home port. On the other hand, if you will be dividing your time equally between home and cruising, or even living aboard full-time, and cruising will include long distances to the islands or to Mexico

FIGURE 1–1.   *This Hatteras 54 motor yacht exemplifies the trend toward large—and luxurious—cruising boats.* (*Courtesy Hatteras Yachts*)

perhaps, then you might easily feel the need for the 50-footer with its huge capacity for fuel, water, and stores.

Length overall, however, does not tell the whole story in how big a boat really is. Her displacement is the more telling figure. When someone hears that our boat, *Duchess*, is 44 feet long, they often say "Oh, what a big boat!" But I don't think she's big at all, since her narrow (by today's standards) beam, shoal draft, and underbody configuration combine to give her a displacement of only 20,950 pounds. Compare the data for *Duchess*, a Solarium 44, and that of a Krogen 42, at 39,500 pounds. The Solarium is the "longer" boat, and the layouts are similar in that both have a main saloon, a galley, a separate pilot house, two staterooms, and two heads. Both are displacement hulls (more on this later) with a single engine, and both have approximately the same cruising speed. But look at the difference in tankage. The Krogen carries almost three times the amount of fuel and close to twice the amount of water. What is less apparent from just looking at drawings and statistics is the increase in storage space aboard the Krogen, and the overall feeling of greater "elbow room" that she provides. So the shorter boat is, in reality, almost twice the size of the longer one.

A larger boat naturally means greater expense, and not just in initial cost. Bigger engines mean higher fuel costs, added gear will often mean bigger and therefore more pricey items, and repair and maintenance costs are higher.

A larger boat also means more work, although I wouldn't necessarily say that a larger boat is all that much harder to handle. A 50-footer equipped with a bow thruster may slide into a skinny opening at the dock with greater ease than a 35-footer if there's a current running or it's a windy day. Still, heavier gear is harder to handle, and more space means more to clean, more to varnish, and more to maintain.

So big is not always better, unless it happens to be what you want. It does mean more room, more carrying capacity, often more comfort both in a seaway and at anchor, and, of course, more cost and more work. Only you can decide how big you want, and how much you are willing to pay for it.

HULL TYPE

There are basically three types of powerboat hulls: displacement, semi-displacement, and planing. The most common type in production boats today is the semi-displacement hull (Figure 1-2). Like everything else, there are advantages and disadvantages to each.

A displacement boat is one that remains *in* the water—it *displaces* an amount of water equal to its weight—as opposed to a planing hull, which can climb partially out of the water. Displacement hulls can be either round-bilge or hard chine (V-bottom). I think the main reason they are less popular today is that their speed is limited to their hull speed. The formula for determining hull speed is the square root of the waterline length multiplied by 1.25 (this figure varies; some designers go as high as 1.4) equals hull speed in knots. This gives our *Duchess* a speed of around 8 to 8½ knots and no more. If you try to push a displacement hull beyond her hull speed, the boat will squat at the stern, push a huge bow wave, use enormous amounts of fuel, and all for a fraction of a knot increase. If the boat is operating at an efficient speed, she should be leaving virtually

FIGURE 1–2.   *The Sabreline 36, with 18-knot cruising speeds, is typical of the modern "performance" trawler.* (*Courtesy Sabre Yachts*)

no wake. As a rule, this most efficient speed is something less than hull speed.

So why have a displacement boat? Because in terms of seaworthiness, they can't be beat. The working trawlers (the basis for our "trawler yachts"), offshore fishing boats that stay at sea for days at a time, and ocean-going tugs, all are displacement craft. They are the most economical boats to operate in terms of fuel, and in rough seas are easier to handle than a semi-displacement or planing hull. Their long, straight, and usually deep keel gives them greater directional stability, particularly at slow speeds (Figure 1-3); and a true passage-maker will generally be ballasted as well.

The single propeller and large rudder also add to the boats' ease of handling at low speeds and in rough conditions, plus the rudder and aperture offer protection to the propeller in shallow waters. We have on a few occasions run over a crab-pot line and held our breath watching the buoy bounce along the side of the hull as the line slid along the keel, past the rudder, and bounced into the stern wake with no harm to pot or boat. With the exposed propeller of a twin-screw installation, the line would likely have wrapped itself around the prop and brought all systems to a screeching halt.

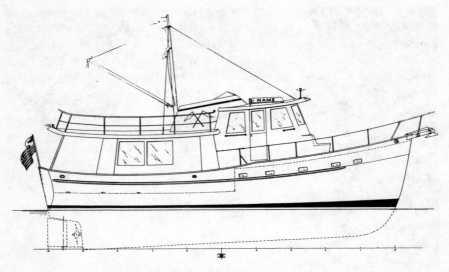

FIGURE 1–3. *The Krogen 42's long, straight keel, single propeller and large rudder combine to give her both directional stability and ease of handling at low speeds as well as in rough seas.* (*Courtesy Kadey-Krogen Yachts, Inc.*)

It's true that a twin-screw installation can give a boat tremendous maneuverability in close quarters, by using the engine controls rather than the wheel, but this is not the same as the overall handling ability at slow speeds, where a single propeller on-center and a large rudder are superior.

Many consider twin engines a safety feature, and there is some merit in this. It does assume, of course, that whatever the problem is it will only affect one engine, not both. I have seen a few boats with two engines coupled to a single shaft, but these were very large yachts and it's not a practical arrangement for most medium-sized cruisers. For boats under 30 feet, an outboard can sometimes be used as an emergency come-home engine, and larger boats may be able to use a dinghy with a large outboard as a yawl boat, but this is only practical for a short distance in calm conditions, and even then it may not be good enough. Another alternative is a take-off that will allow the generator to be used as an emergency engine. The best measures are preventive—treat your engine as if your life depended on it, because it just might.

A planing boat, by virtue of its hull design and tremendous amounts of power, is able to lift itself partially out of the water and skim along the surface, and is therefore capable of very high speeds. Without a keel, they lack directional stability. A planing boat used for cruising should have at least a moderate keel to improve its tracking ability. In theory, with a planing boat you should be able to pick your conditions and go fast enough to make port before bad weather sets in. In practice, we all know how fickle the weather can be, and sooner or later you're going to get caught. Many planing boats will start to slam in really rough water, forcing you to slow down at the very time when the boat needs all the sea-keeping qualities she can get.

The compromise between seakindliness and the desire for speed is the semi-displacement (or semi-planing, if you prefer) hull. With the exception of those few people whose cruising plans include ocean-crossing passagemaking, a semi-displacement boat can be a pretty good compromise. With a keel, even a shallow one, it is better-handling at low speeds than a pure planing boat, although more power is needed to get it up onto plane, and its top speed will be less. The twin engines aid maneuverability and are a safety feature. Semi-displacement boats are not, unfortunately, economical at high speeds, and for that reason most cruisers I know run their boats at, or a little above, hull speed most of the time. With two engines, of course, even at hull speed you are still burning almost twice the fuel.

ENGINES

We've already discussed single vs. twin screw, but there is still the choice of diesel or gasoline, and inboard or outboard. Small cruisers (under 30 feet) are often equipped with outboard or sterndrive (inboard/outboard or I/O) engines. These are usually gasoline engines, but as diesels become more compact you are more apt to see a small diesel installed with an outboard drive unit. They do allow more room for living space below decks and that can be important on a small cruising boat; however, fuel tankage plus the size of the boat limits them to local cruising grounds.

For most long-range cruisers, there is no question but that the engine is inboard and the fuel is diesel. Many manufacturers do offer the choice between gas or diesel, however, so we should at least consider the options. Gas engines are definitely less expensive; diesels can cost two or three times as much. We looked at one 48-footer with twin engines that cost an additional $50,000 for diesel instead of gasoline. That's a lot of money.

Initial cost aside, three factors make diesel the overwhelming choice: economy of operation, safety, and reliability. I remember when at-the-pump diesel prices were much lower than gasoline, but all that proves today is my age. Although in most places diesel is now the higher-priced fuel, because of the greater efficiency of the diesel engine, fuel costs will be roughly half that of a gas engine.

Gasoline is a much more volatile fuel than diesel. A gas-engine installation calls for a ventilation system with blowers to eliminate any gas fumes, and an automatic fire-extinguishing system is a must. Ventilation and fire extinguishers are important with a diesel installation as well, but nowhere near as critical. It's true that almost all boats carry gasoline, anyway—for the dinghy's outboard—but both engine and fuel tank are out in the open air, not in a closed-off compartment inside the boat.

Diesels are far and away the most reliable engines. Given reasonable care, they just go on and on and on. About the only thing that will stop a diesel completely is bad fuel, and there are ways to prevent this, which we'll discuss in detail in the chapter on the power plant. Gasoline engines, on the other hand, are more complicated and more prone to a myriad of little problems that can cause you much aggravation.

HULL MATERIAL

The overwhelming majority of production boats today are built of fiberglass. It is a good, strong hull material, but now that the age of blistering is upon us, it can no longer be called a maintenance-free miracle product. Blistering occurs when moisture is absorbed between the gelcoat and the laminate, or into the laminate itself. In a survey conducted in 1987 by *Practical Sailor* magazine, it was found that an average of 27 percent of all boats had developed blistering problems. The spread ranged from 10 percent of the boats in the northeast to 50 percent in southern waters. Both the warm water temperatures and the fact that boats are generally left in the water year-round contributed to the higher numbers.

Every company has their own different way of preventing

blistering—some more successfully than others. At this writing, one of the more common techniques is to back up the gelcoat with a laminate using vinylester resin. Boats built in this way have been around for five years now and are showing little, if any, blistering problems. There are also water-resistant gelcoats, such as Blister Guard from Glidden, that are being used with success. The drawback to the new gelcoats is that they are designed for underwater use and do not hold up well on the topsides, so builders must use different gelcoats for above and below the water, making it a costly process. Applying an epoxy barrier coat is another method, and one that is often used for older boats that have developed blisters.

While I would not hesitate to buy another fiberglass boat, I would investigate the construction methods carefully and check out the reputation of the builder before I made the purchase. Talk to other owners and find out what kind of problems they have encountered, and the attitude of the company in dealing with those problems. Horror stories of lawsuits and disreputable dealers abound, and boats from some manufacturers seem to have far fewer blistering problems than others. Meanwhile, we know that extensive research is underway, fiberglass boats are getting better and better, and hopefully blistering will soon be a thing of the past.

Other boatbuilding materials include steel and aluminum. Steel is one of the strongest yet heaviest materials. There are only a handful of production boatbuilders working in steel in this country, more in Europe, and they are primarily large yachts or workboats. Houseboats are likely to be steel or aluminum. There are also quite a few custom builders who specialize in steel and aluminum construction. Maintenance needn't be higher on a metal boat than on any other material, but it's not something you can ignore either. You can put off waxing the topsides of a fiberglass boat until it's dull and chalky with no real harm done, but delay painting a steel boat for that long and you're inviting rust and corrosion problems. Electrolysis is probably the biggest enemy of both steel and aluminum, and constant vigilance is required.

Wood is still a viable boatbuilding material, but your choice here will be an older, used boat or a custom one. Traditional plank-on-frame construction does mean high maintenance, as well as less interior space than a similar-size fiberglass boat. Newer methods, however, can give us the best of both worlds. *Duchess* was built using the Gougeon brothers' W.E.S.T. system of epoxy saturation, giving us a hull that is light, strong, and impervious to rot or worms, while cabins and interior have the warmth and beauty of traditional wood construction.

There are some lovely powerboats on the market today, and there are also some that are real pieces of junk. At the last Miami Boat Show, I went aboard a well-advertised boat, "designed for cruising," resplendent in Euro-styled glitz. A friend who was with me leaned against a bulkhead, and it actually moved under his weight. Walking around on deck also revealed a decided amount of "give." I didn't bother to check the hull-to-deck joint, but if it had been well-bonded and through-bolted I would have been surprised. The point here is simply that there is a lot more to a cruising boat than wood trim, stylish decoration, and lots of goodies. A cruising boat must stand up to hard and constant use in all kinds of weather. Poke around, ask questions, visit the factory if you can. Hiring a surveyor is always a good idea, too, even for a new boat.

NEW OR USED

Remember the last energy crisis, when there were long lines at the gas station, sailors looked smug, and you could buy a powerboat for a pittance? Those days are just a memory, and powerboats are more than holding their own. This is not to say that you can't get good value in a used powerboat, because you certainly can.

The main reason most people shop for a used boat instead of a new one is cost. The purchase price of a used boat will be cheaper than the same boat new, plus you're getting lots of extras—docklines, fenders, ground tackle, canvas work, and usually at least some electronics. All these extras can add significantly to the base price of a new boat.

Even though you are getting extras with a used boat, you are getting someone else's choice of the ideal extra, whatever it may be. And while a lot of the "bugs" will have been worked out, you may also have some unwelcome changes to deal with. The boat may have a vertical windlass, while you prefer a horizontal one, for instance, or the interior may be decorated in flaming floral fuchsia. If you know that changes must be made, then figure the cost as part of the "real" price of the boat. With a new boat, you may be paying full price for the extras, but at least you will be getting exactly what you want.

The basic question, of course, is what shape is the boat in, and what is the condition of all that used gear? A new boat is presumably under warranty, and all new gear you buy for her will have some sort of guarantee as well. When you buy a used boat, you buy her "as is." While I think a survey is a good idea for a new boat, it is downright foolhardy to buy a used boat without one.

It is easiest to get both financing and insurance coverage for a new boat. Both banks and insurance companies will insist on a survey before they will make a commitment on a used boat, and the surveyor will have to be someone on their approved list. Many banks also insist that a boat be documented. This is not a problem with a new boat, particularly a new-production boat, but it can be a real headache with an older boat that has never been documented and has been through numerous owners.

So far I've been focusing on used boats that are still fairly modern. The other possibility is a much older, wooden boat. These are often a real bargain in terms of price, but they can mean an awful lot of work and a high price tag in the long run. The last time we were in the Bahamas, we met a couple cruising on their beautifully restored Elco. They had cruised the length of both U.S. coasts, shipped her to Europe for a two-year cruise of the canals, and were then heading down-island to South America. They had purchased the boat in California for "only" $16,000. Two years later, they had virtually rebuilt the entire boat from stem to stern, and had spent an additional $150,000. Was it worth it? They thought so, and no one can argue with that. She was exactly what they wanted, and they were completely happy with her.

The other type of boat to consider is one that is custom built. Again, this can be an expensive proposition, but it is a way to have everything exactly the way *you* want it. We were able to afford *Duchess* by doing much of the interior and finish work ourselves, and Taz worked full-time with the builder on the hull, cabin trunks, and the roughed-in interior. This meant, however, giving up several years of cruising in order to do the work. We enjoy boatbuilding, so the process was worth it for us, but obviously this is not everyone's cup of tea. If your goal is to go cruising immediately, then buy the finished product. Many companies do offer choices of arrangements and styles so you can customize to a certain extent, particularly with the larger boats.

CABIN LAYOUTS

Individual requirements vary so much that it is both impractical and impossible to describe an "ideal" layout. Now is the time to give serious thought as to how you will cruise, where you will cruise, and who you will cruise with. Will it be just you and your spouse with an occasional guest or two, or with a passel of children or frequent guests? Do you plan on long passages to out-of-the-way places, necessitating ample tankage and stowage capacity, or will it be short hops between civilized areas where supplies are readily available? Are you cruising to the tropics, north where it's rainy and cold, or both? It's a good idea to make a list of everything you would like in your "ideal" cruising boat, then keep the list handy when you're looking at plans or going to a boat show. See how many boats measure up, and where you will have to compromise.

The Saloon

When not underway, this is where you'll spend most of your time. It is your living room, often your dining room, sometimes a workroom, and the place you go to relax and to entertain guests. Ample and comfortable seating is a must, and it's also nice to have a place to stretch out to read a book, watch TV, or take a nap (Figure 1-4).

An L-shaped settee with a hi-lo table is a common arrangement on many powerboats. The table is designed to be a dining table in the high position, a coffee table in the low position, and to convert the settee to a double berth. Like many multiple-function items, they do all the jobs but none of them particularly well. Consider your dining table at home. You can pull your chair right up to it and sit quite close and quite comfortably (Figure 1-5). But a convertible table stops at the edge of the settee so the table can be lowered, forcing diners to sit forward on the edge of their seats. If it were *just* a dining table, it could extend over the settee by several inches and be much more comfortable. In the coffee table position, it must have a dropleaf or there will be no legroom at all.

In order to answer that most-asked question at boat shows— "How many will she sleep?"—most settees will convert to a berth. This is, in my opinion, an overrated and useless feature. There should be *no* permanent sleeping quarters in the saloon. At best, it could be

FIGURE 1–4.   *The saloon of the Krogen 42* Joan M *has a comfortable sofa to starboard. (Port side is shown in Figure 1–5.)*

FIGURE 1–5.   *These armchairs flank the fold-up dining table as well as serving as additional seating for the saloon. Also note the handhold running the length of the overhead.*

for an occasional overnight guest, but they would have no privacy and their sleeping hours would be dictated by everyone else in the crew. This is especially difficult if the saloon-berth occupants are youngsters and the adults want to stay up past the kid's bedtime. There may be no getting around this if you opt for a small boat, but it is far from an ideal arrangement.

Powerboat saloons are generally wide, spacious, bright and airy places to be, with plenty of elbow room. But the wide-openness means they should have handholds on the overhead, running the length of the saloon, so anyone moving through the boat in a seaway can do so easily and safely.

Staterooms

People over six feet tall often have a real problem finding a boat with a comfortable berth. The standard is generally 6 feet 6 inches, which doesn't leave a lot of room for a pillow or for toe wiggling. You're most likely to find a long berth in an aft cabin on a medium-to-large yacht, where it may even be a queen-sized bed to rival the one at home. The only way to know if it fits, or if it's comfortable, is to stretch out and see for yourself. Cushions should be a minimum of 5 inches, 6 is better.

There should be a dresser, or at least a shelf, next to the bunk, so you'll have a place for a cup of coffee, reading glasses, books, all the paraphernalia we seem to need when we go to bed. And it should go without saying that there must be sitting headroom over the bunk, so you can sit up to read or sit down to tie your shoes.

Adequate ventilation is also very important. Installing a fan can help, but it's better to have opening ports and a hatch, or at least a pair of dorade vents. If the boat has air-conditioning, this won't matter, except that many people like to shut down the generator at night and that won't be possible if you can't get some fresh air into the cabin on a steamy night.

The Galley

Every cruising powerboat has the basics—sink, stove, refrigerator—but what is often lacking is counter space. We were on one boat where the only counter was a folding cover that fit over the stove. It was fine when we were just making sandwiches, but impossible when we actually wanted to cook; and this was on a 37-footer billed as a cruising boat. In my opinion, it was only a cruising boat if we were cruising from restaurant to restaurant.

One trend I've noticed on newer boats is to install a countertop range with no oven, along with a combination microwave/convection oven that will bake and broil as well as microwave. It's an idea that's great in theory but terrible in practice, because the inside dimensions are *tiny*. You can make toast, but forget about baking a loaf of bread. You can broil chicken pieces, but you can't bake a whole chicken, let alone a turkey if you're cruising at Thanksgiving or Christmas. A microwave oven is a fine addition to a galley, but it cannot replace a conventional oven, no matter how much space is saved.

Cooktops should have rails to keep pots secure when underway, and all counters need fiddles to prevent bowls and utensils from sliding onto the cabin sole (Figure 1-6). Sleek, smooth, uninterrupted countertops may be lovely in the showroom, but they are totally impractical on a true cruising boat. Fiddles on a dining table, however, are best if they are removable, since they can get in the way when the table is used for other activities.

Head Compartment

The head compartment should provide privacy, plenty of elbow room, good ventilation, and surfaces that are easy to clean. Ideally, the shower should be a separate stall, although this is not always possible on smaller boats. On boats with two heads, at least one usually has a separate shower.

It's really not all that bad if the shower is not separate, as long as there is plenty of room to move around. A shower curtain can be mounted so it slides around to protect cabinets and toilet from splashing water.

Hand-held shower heads are common, and they should be fitted with an on/off button. Otherwise, they waste an inordinate amount of water. You can, of course, just turn off the water while you soap up, but then you must readjust the hot and cold water when you turn it back on. With the on/off button on the shower head, you only have to adjust it once.

FIGURE 1—6.   *This well-thought-out galley has ample counter space with fiddles all around, both microwave and conventional oven, and plenty of cabinets and drawers. (Courtesy Hatteras Yachts)*

Navigation Station

On boats with a separate pilot house, there is generally plenty of room to lay out a chart as well as space for compass, radio and other instruments. If the steering station is in the saloon, however, then some living and storage space must be allocated for ship's business. All instruments are usually arranged on a console in front of the wheel, but somewhere close by there must also be room to completely spread out a chart, and there needs to be handy storage for all the books, cruising guides, tide tables, parallels, pencils and other equipment necessary to navigation.

The dining table is often pressed into service, but if you find it's not convenient you might want to consider installing a flip-up chart table next to the helm.

Engine Room

This is the heart of a cruising powerboat, although the cook may argue the point. It needs to be easily accessible; if it's not, it becomes all too tempting to put off routine maintenance for another day. Only large yachts have the luxury of an actual door leading to the engine room, but if the engines are beneath the saloon sole—a common arrangement—then you should not have to move any furniture to get to the hatches, and the hatches should be as big as possible.

It's important that there is ample space all around the engine. Sometimes the engine is jammed right up against a forward bulkhead, making it an effort in frustration to reach the front of the engine.

Not just the engine, but all equipment installed in the compartment should be easy to get to for service and repairs. If at all possible, try to fit in a workbench, and storage space for tools and spare parts.

TOPSIDES LAYOUT

If you've ever inched your way forward on a stormy night to check the anchor, clutching the handrail and toes curled around the deck edge, praying you don't get blown overboard, then you already appreciate the importance of wide side decks. I would willingly give up some interior space to be able to move around topsides in safety and comfort.

And anyplace you go topsides, there should be *something* for you to grab on to—either a handrail or a lifeline. Lifelines should be 30 inches to 36 inches high. Any lower and they are more likely to flip you overboard than keep you safe if you fall against them.

All hardware—handrails, lifeline stanchions, cleats, windlass, everything—should be bedded, through-bolted, and installed with a solid backing plate. Simply screwing hardware to the deck is not enough.

In good weather, you'll be spending a considerable amount of time topside, so look for comfortable seating, room to stretch out for a nap or sunbathing, and a place to install a table if there isn't one already. A lot of us, however, are no longer thrilled at the idea of hours and hours in the sunshine and insist on at least a partially shaded lounging area—either a structural cover or a canvas awning that can be rolled in or out.

Shade is often wanted, too, on the fly bridge. In southern waters you can quickly fry yourself to a crisp without the protection of a bimini. A few small powerboats, advertised as cruising boats, offer the fly bridge as the only steering station. This is ridiculous. In bad weather, unless the area can be completely enclosed with a windowed canvas arrangement, you might as well be in a sailboat.

If most of your steering is done from a fly bridge, give some serious thought to providing space for at least a folded chart. And you'll need some arrangement—shock cord perhaps, or a hinged lexan cover—to keep it from blowing away. It will save a lot of trips up and down the ladder to the dining table to figure out where you are.

Choosing a cruising boat is a pursuit filled with as many headaches as joys. Yet once that agonizing decision is made, it always seems to be downhill from there. Getting ready for a cruise is so much fun, and cruising itself even more fun, that all those early frustrations are soon forgotten—left behind in a bubbling wake as you head out for new horizons and new adventures.

CHAPTER 2

The Power Plant

IT'S ALWAYS INTERESTING asking boat manufacturers to describe what they consider as today's typical cruising powerboat buyer. Builders of semi-displacement and planing boats reply that their customers are successful, busy people who enjoy cruising but don't have as much time as they might like to indulge in it. They believe the current trend is for faster boats, ones that will get their owners where they want to go in a hurry, so they can have more time to "be there" and still get home in time for work.

Displacement-boat builders, on the other hand, say the trend is for slow, heavy cruising boats with long-range capability at economical fuel costs. Their customers are tired of the hustle and bustle of everyday living and want to slow down, enjoy the scenery, and smell the water lilies. Dudley Boycott, who cruises (at around 6½ knots) with his wife Rose aboard their 36-foot Marine Trader, says when he's on the boat he is where he wants to be, so why rush?

Both viewpoints could be right, but the one fact that's for sure is that the choice between displacement, semi-displacement, and planing hulls, and the choice between single engine and twin screw, are among the biggest decisions a boat owner must make. The questions are: how fast is "fast," how much horsepower is needed, and at what price? We touched on this in the first chapter, but I think it warrants further discussion.

POWER REQUIREMENTS

A displacement boat, as described in the first chapter, is so called because it remains *in* the water—it displaces an amount of water equal to its weight, is limited in speed by its wave length. Wave length is the distance between one wave crest and the following one, and as the distance increases so does the speed. A displacement boat reaches hull speed when its wave length—the distance between the bow wave and the stern wave—is equal to its waterline length. Obviously, the longer a boat is on the waterline, the faster it is capable of going.

Keep in mind, though, that hull speed is a theoretical figure, and displacement boats rarely cruise consistently at that speed. With a freshly painted bottom, and in perfectly smooth water, a boat may reach hull speed fairly easily, but this is seldom the case. Most often, something between 75 percent and 80 percent of hull speed proves to be the most economical and the most comfortable speed. I spent one summer crewing for a fisherman who owned an old wooden displacement boat. By the end of the day he'd be in a hurry to get home and would start cranking up the rpm's. As the boat approached hull speed, a perceptible vibration would begin. When she hit hull speed, we all knew it, because the vibration was bad enough to knock us off our feet and I always expected the engine to jump right off its beds. It was hard on the crew, harder on the boat, and wasted tremendous amounts of fuel.

Still, even if a displacement boat is pushed to its limit, it takes a surprisingly small amount of horsepower to do it. Francis Kinney, in *Skene's Elements of Yacht Design*, gives the formula for figuring required horsepower. Using *Duchess*, a 40-foot waterline powerboat, as an example, let's see how big an engine she really needs.

In Chapter 1 we figured her hull speed (square root of the waterline length multiplied by a speed-length ratio of 1.3): 40 × 1.3 = 8.22 knots.

Using the chart in Figure 2-1, we go from 1.3 speed-length ratio at

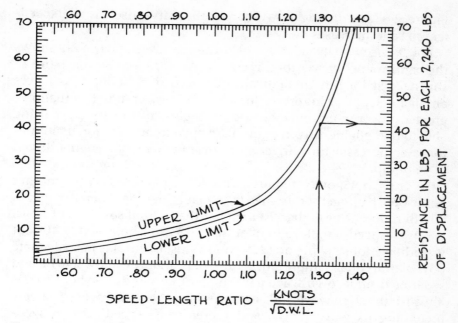

FIGURE 2–1. *Curves covering range of resistance for displacement hulls. (Courtesy* Skene's Elements of Yacht Design *by Francis S. Kinney, © 1981 by Dodd, Mead & Company, Inc.)*

the bottom up to a little above the lower limit (since *Duchess* is fairly light displacement), and find that the resistance is 42 pounds for each long ton (2,240 pounds) of displacement. Her displacement, 20,950 pounds, divided by 2,240, equals 9.35 long tons. So the resistance is 9.35 × 42 = 393 pounds.

Effective horsepower (EHP) is found by the formula *EHP = resistance × speed × .003*. For *Duchess*, EHP = 393 × 8.22 × .003 = 9.7 HP.

Now the efficiency (or inefficiency) of the propeller must be taken into account. A three-blade propeller on a powerboat is figured at 60 to 66 percent efficiency. Taking the lower figure: 9.7 divided by .60 = 16 shaft horsepower needed to achieve a hull speed of 8.2 knots. It is common practice to add an additional 33 percent for running in poor conditions, which brings us to a required shaft horsepower (shp) of 22. That's for hull speed; if we run the boat at around 75 percent of hull speed—six knots—less than 5 shp is required. This incredible difference is explained by looking again at the resistance chart in

Figure 2-1 and noting how sharply the curve rises as the speed-length ratio increases.

For *Duchess*, we installed a 44-hp Yanmar diesel. Figure 2-2 shows the performance curves for this engine. At 2000 rpm we reach the 22 shp needed for our theoretical hull speed of 8 knots. This leaves ample horsepower in reserve for a burst of power in tight situations, greater power in extreme weather, and gives us the option of being able to add engine-driven equipment such as an additional alternator, a compressor for refrigeration, or an emergency engine-driven bilge pump.

Figuring out power requirements for a planing boat is another kettle of fish altogether. In theory, a boat is planing when her speed-length ratio is 2 or higher. Remember that with displacement hulls, we use a speed-length ratio of around 1.3. So a boat with a 40-foot waterline should plane at 12.7 knots. This assumes it has adequate power and, equally important, a hull shape that will allow it to lift and separate from its own wave pattern; in other words, the boat moves ahead of the stern wave and begins to climb the bow wave, effectively increasing its wave length and therefore its speed. This is well-illustrated by the photographs of a 32-foot Nordic Tug. In Figure 2-3,

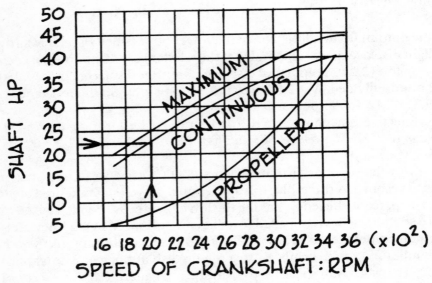

FIGURE 2–2. *Performance curve for Yanmar 44-hp diesel.*

FIGURE 2–3. *The 32-foot Nordic Tug only looks traditional—she is capable of speeds up to 16.8 knots. Here the boat's speed is below hull speed. Note that the bow wave is barely visible and there is almost no stern wave. (Courtesy Nordic Tugs, Inc.)*

the tug's speed is below hull speed. The bow wave is barely visible and there is almost no stern wave. A similar tug, in Figure 2-4, has broken through the hull-speed barrier and is moving at planing speed. The bow has risen and the boat has clearly moved ahead of her stern wave.

There are formulas for figuring required horsepower for planing boats, but there are so many variables involved that they are of more use to the designer, who has sufficient data on a great number of similar boats, than they are to a buyer looking at one specific boat. Many manufacturers do offer a choice of engines, with the bigger engines naturally giving higher top speeds.

It's worth noting the differences in fuel consumption between a displacement boat with a single engine, and a semi-displacement one with twin engines. Table 2-1 shows fuel consumption at various speeds and rpms for a semi-displacement 40-footer with twin 250-hp diesels. A displacement boat of similar length, with a smaller 135-hp diesel, uses around 2.8 gallons per hour at a cruising speed of 8 knots.

In case you're wondering why the displacement boat has a 135-hp

FIGURE 2—4.   *Another 32-foot Nordic Tug. In this shot the boat has broken through the hull-speed barrier and is moving onto plane. The bow has risen and the boat has clearly moved ahead of her stern wave.* (*Courtesy Nordic Tugs, Inc.*)

engine, and *Duchess*, with the same waterline length, has 44 hp, it's because this boat has over twice the displacement with 3 feet more beam and deeper draft. All these factors must be taken into account, since they do have an effect on power requirements and handling characteristics.

It remains, however, that if the semi-displacement boat travels at a displacement speed of 8 knots, it is still burning almost twice the fuel simply because two engines are operating instead of one. Although

Table 2-1
FUEL CONSUMPTION FOR SEMI-DISPLACEMENT 40-FOOT CRUISER
WITH TWIN 250-HP DIESELS

Engine RPMs	Knots	Gallons/Hour
2400	15.5	20
2200	12.0	15
1800	9.0	9
1500	8.0	6.5
1400	7.0	5

these figures are from actual speed trials, they are given as generalities, since both speed and fuel consumption can vary greatly, even between identical boats and identical engines. Wind and sea conditions, whether the boat has a dirty bottom or a clean one, whether she is light in the water or loaded for cruising, whether the engine is in good condition or needs work—these are but a few of the factors that can make a significant difference.

We tend to think of semi-displacement boats as having two engines, and while most of them do, there are some (such as the Nordic Tug) that have only one engine, on-center with a deep keel and protected prop, yet with enough power to get up onto a plane. Often this is achieved by installing a turbocharged diesel instead of the more common naturally aspirated engine.

Basically a diesel's power is derived from the amount of air that can be drawn into the engine—if it can get more air, it can burn more fuel and therefore deliver more power. On a naturally aspirated engine, air is forced into the cylinders by the movement of the pistons. A turbocharged engine uses the exhaust gases to drive a blower that forces more air into the engine, thereby greatly increasing its power (Table 2-2). *Duchess*'s 44 hp Yanmar, if fitted with a turbocharger, would deliver 55 hp from the same basic engine. Most turbocharged engines are also equipped with an intercooler to reduce the intake air temperature and increase the engine's efficiency—and power—even more. Table 2-2 shows top speeds achieved, and average fuel consumption, for a 32-foot semi-displacement boat with a single naturally aspirated engine, a turbocharged engine, and a turbocharger with an intercooler.

Table 2-2
FUEL CONSUMPTION FOR A 32-FOOT SEMI-DISPLACEMENT CRUISING BOAT WITH DIFFERENT TYPES OF ENGINES

Engine	Top Speed	Approx. Gallons/Hour
120-HP Naturally Aspirated Diesel	12.0	2.40
140-HP Turbocharged Diesel	13.7	2.65
175-HP Turbocharged with Intercooler	16.8	3.40

Turbocharging can tremendously increase the power output of a given engine, but it is a complicated system with close tolerances. While a knowledgeable owner can perform most, if not all, of the maintenance and repair of a naturally aspirated diesel, problems with a turbocharger may require calling in an expert, and experts are not always easy to find in out-of-the-way cruising ports.

INSTRUMENTS

Believe it or not, some engine manufacturers still make instrument panels with warning lights instead of gauges. These appropriately called "idiot lights" may be acceptable on a sailboat where the engine is rarely used, but on a powerboat you must be able to monitor what is happening down in the engine room at all times, and only a gauge that can be read will do. By the time a warning light comes on, it is usually too late to avoid trouble—it's already happening. Of course, if you often have someone with a short attention span on the helm, it's not a bad idea to have both—a red light or a buzzer might catch their attention if they are ignoring the dials.

Normal instruments include those for oil pressure, cooling water temperature, a tachometer, an engine hour meter, and an ammeter instead of just a charging light. Aside from these, there is a myriad of other instrumentation available (Figure 2-5). A speedometer and distance log can be added, and I prefer a log that includes a resettable "leg distance" in addition to the total distance covered. A rudder-angle indicator is always helpful, particularly on boats with hydraulic steering. A turbo gauge will monitor pressure buildup on a turbocharged engine. And on boats with twin engines, an engine synchronizer is invaluable.

While alarm gauges are a good idea, particularly for oil pressure and water temperature, it is bad practice to install an automatic shutdown feature. Charter boat owners may feel it is a way of protecting their valuable investment, but cruising boat owners should be able to make the choice between shutting down or risking damage to the engine if it should become necessary in an emergency.

Other alarms could include ones for high water in the bilge, and for fire. Every engine room should be fitted with an automatic fire extinguisher, such as one of the Coast Guard–approved Halon systems (Figure 2-6). These can be fitted with an alarm so you'll

FIGURE 2–5.   *There is a myriad of engine instruments available. This Jefferson 37 shows a typical installation.*

FIGURE 2–6.   *An automatic fire extinguisher, like this Coast Guard-approved Halon system, should be installed in every engine room.*

know at once if it goes off; and unlike shutdown systems for oil pressure or water temperature, you might want to consider installing an automatic shutdown feature that will work in conjunction with the Halon system. The Halon will put out the fire, but if a diesel engine continues to run it will quickly remove all the Halon from the compartment. Since diesels operate at a high temperature, the Halon could be removed before the temperature in the engine room had lowered sufficiently and a reflash of the fire could occur. Fireboy's engine shutdown system (Figure 2-7) will handle up to three engines and is equipped with an override switch.

As fine as all these gauges and alarms are, nothing can take the place of a visual inspection of the ship and all her systems. You need an established, written checklist to go through each time you leave the dock, and a routine of periodic inspections while underway.

VENTILATION

For safety reasons, a compartment for a gasoline engine must have at least two ventilator ducts and a bilge blower to ensure removal of

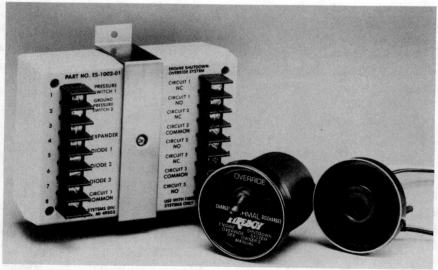

FIGURE 2—7. *Fireboy's engine shutdown system will handle up to three engines and is equipped with an override switch. (Courtesy Fireboy Halon Systems Division, Convenience Marine Products, Inc.)*

explosive gasses. If the batteries are kept in the engine compartment, as is common, ventilation is important to prevent the buildup of hydrogen gas that forms when the batteries are being charged. This can be especially critical if the batteries are accidentally overcharged.

It is not a Coast Guard requirement that diesel engine space be ventilated (it is required for gas engines), but it is still important. A diesel requires tremendous amounts of fresh air to operate efficiently. According to Nigel Calder in *Marine Diesel Engines*, a naturally aspirated diesel needs almost 1,500 cubic feet of air to burn one gallon of fuel; turbocharged engines need almost twice that. Diesel installation manuals generally recommend that at least one air intake duct and a forced discharge ventilator be installed in the engine room.

Air intake is usually accomplished by using cowl vents or clamshell ventilators; flexible vent tubing can be added to direct the airflow around obstructions or through bulkheads if necessary. A bilge blower should be one that's Coast Guard approved and designed specifically for engine room installation.

ENGINE MAINTENANCE

It is not within the scope of this book to go into a detailed step-by-step procedure of engine maintenance. Such care is spelled out in each engine's owner's manual, and there are several books available devoted entirely to the subject. There are certain points, however, that should be emphasized for cruising-boat owners, since they are the ones frequently out of reach of their local mechanic.

Certainly anyone who goes cruising should have at least a rudimentary knowledge of how the engine works and be able to perform routine maintenance without calling for help. Of all the cruising couples I know, almost without exception it is the man who does the engine work. This arrangement is fine with me; I hate getting greasy. As a naval architect I did learn about speccing various engines for different boats, and their installation and engine-room layouts. But all the theory in the world cannot replace digging in and doing things yourself. So I have changed the oil in the engine, changed the fuel filters, and bled the fuel system. I've read the manual, asked questions, and helped Taz whenever I could. Why? Because if something should happen to him, I want to feel confident that I can get us, and the boat, safely back to port.

The vast majority of diesel engine problems can be traced to a single source: dirty fuel. If you can keep dirt and water out of the fuel, right from the start, you are going a long way toward having a trouble-free relationship with your engines.

Vigilance starts at the fuel dock. When filling the tanks, always use a funnel with a mesh screen to filter out contaminants. If you see a lot of gunk building up on the screen, you're better off going to another fuel dock—assuming that there *is* another fuel dock.

Always try to keep the fuel tanks topped up, particularly if the boat is going to sit for a while. If the tank is not full, condensation will form at the top and the water will mix with the fuel where it can cause untold wear and damage to the engine's fuel injection system. Water is heavier than diesel fuel; it and dirt particles will eventually settle to the bottom of the tank, right at the fuel pickup. Algae loves to grow in this mess, creating even more problems.

Some custom boats have tanks with a sump at the bottom, below the fuel pickup, where water and contaminants can be drained off or samples can be taken, but this is rarely the case with stock boats. The fuel pickup is generally installed a couple of inches above the bottom of the tank, but you do need to check the fuel periodically, to see if you are getting a buildup of water or sludge. Most mechanics recommend against using any kind of a fuel additive, so the only solution for a badly contaminated tank is to drain the fuel, clean the tank, and start over.

The best safeguard is the installation of a fuel filter/water separator. The fuel filter on the engine will remove small particles of dirt, but it is not designed to remove the amount of water found in most fuel today. Many of them use a cartridge made of a paper substance that will actually dissolve in water.

A fuel filter/separator is typically mounted on a bulkhead, not on the engine, and does its work before the fuel ever reaches the engine (Figure 2-8). As the fuel passes through the filter, water and heavy contaminants are separated and fall into a clear settling bowl that is fitted with a petcock. They should be checked often, and all water and contaminants drained off.

These filters do an outstanding job, and most boat manufacturers now install one as a matter of course. For a safety measure, it's not a bad idea to install more than one, particularly if you are cruising to areas where the fuel is questionable. I remember when I lived in California boat owners heading for Mexico would routinely install

FIGURE 2–8.　*This pair of fuel filters is installed so one can be shut down while the other one continues to function—allowing servicing while the boat is underway.*

three filter/separators because the fuel in Mexico was so notoriously bad. It's cheap insurance.

Equally important to the life of your engine is clean oil. Changing the oil and filter should be done religiously at the specified times, and the oil should always be of a type that is recommended for your particular engine. Oil formulated for a gasoline engine is not always suitable for a diesel—using the wrong oil can cause considerable damage. When we are leaving for a long cruise, we always put aboard enough engine oil for several changes, knowing full well that the fuel dock or local gas station in a small town is not likely to carry the type that *Duchess* needs.

When you are cruising and underway everyday, then routine maintenance should be performed—every day. Get in the habit of a daily check at the end of each day's run. Check oil and water levels, and visually inspect the fuel filter/water separators—the ones with a glass bowl, such as those made by Racor, make this an easy task. Check the stuffing box on a regular basis. As a rule, it should be tightened so there is just an occasional drip of water from the box. Also check the engine's mounting bolts, and the shaft alignment.

When you are running everyday, you'll quickly become attuned to the sounds and "feel" of the engines, and know almost as a sixth sense when something isn't quite right. A daily inspection will fine-tune this sense, and so will a spotlessly clean engine room. A drop of oil or a splash of rusty water will be instantly apparent on a clean engine, and could pass without notice on a dirty one until serious trouble has developed.

VIBRATION AND NOISE

Every engine vibrates when it's running, and since it is mounted on beds that are attached to the hull, the vibration is transferred to the hull and throughout the boat. If the engine and propeller shaft are properly aligned—and the tolerances are extremely close—the vibration should not be excessive. If it is excessive, check the alignment, and the possibility of a bent propeller shaft. Engines today are generally mounted on flexible rubber mounts, and often have flexible shaft couplings to further reduce vibration (Figure 2-9).

Noise is a fact of life any time the engine is running. And the smaller the boat, the closer you live to the engine, so the more you will notice the noise. Reducing vibration will also reduce noise, but other steps can be taken if it is still greater than you would like.

FIGURE 2–9. *A flexible shaft coupling, like this Aquadrive unit, can reduce vibration to a barely perceptible amount and lessen noise transmission through the hull by as much as 50 percent.* (*Courtesy Aquadrive Systems, Inc.*)

The engine room can be insulated and all cracks and holes plugged—except, of course, ducts for ventilation and exhaust must be left open. Without a doubt, the best noise barrier is sheet lead. The only drawback to lead is the added weight. Soundproofing material, such as that made by Soundown Corporation, is available as a lead/foam composite, a lead/fiberglass composite, and a quilted fiberglass/lead composite. A layer of fiberglass insulation will help a lot, but not as much as the composites. Any material used should be designed *for* engine compartment use; it should be fire retardant and have a covering that will keep it from absorbing fumes.

If the engine is located beneath the cabin sole, simply installing carpeting may do the trick. You can also get carpet underlayment, made of acoustic vinyl and closed-cell foam, that will reduce noise even more.

The noise of a generator is another fact of life on most powerboats, and for those with air-conditioning it can be constant. Insulating the entire engine room is the best solution, but most generator manufacturers can provide enclosures specifically designed for their generators (Figure 2-10).

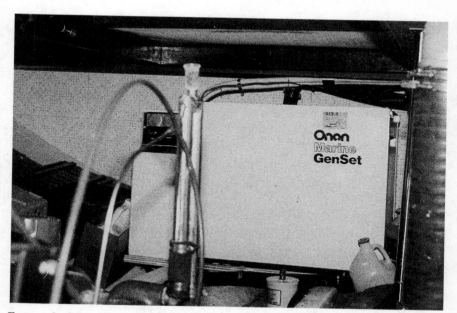

FIGURE 2–10.   *A sound-deadening enclosure designed for a specific generator can greatly reduce the noise level in the engine room.*

Noise from the generator's exhaust is another problem, although this is sometimes more of a problem to other boats than to the folks below with the air conditioner humming away. Onan suggests the following: using a marine muffler, such as the Onan Aqualift; using a flexible exhaust line after the cooling water is injected, or adding a flexible section of line near the exhaust outlet; and installing an exhaust deflector on the outlet to deflect exhaust toward the water.

MAINTENANCE LOG

A good way to ensure that routine maintenance tasks are performed is to keep a log. It doesn't have to be anything fancy; we use a simple spiral notebook. Every time something is done, from changing the oil to a major overhaul, enter the date, the hours on the engine hour meter, and a brief description of what was done. With proper care, a diesel engine will give many years of dependable service.

CHAPTER 3

The Galley

SOME OF THE BEST meals I've ever eaten have been aboard the boat. I don't know that the food is really any better than what we eat ashore. I think it's the atmosphere. All that fresh air and sunshine, the panoramic view of sea and sky, the water lapping against the hull, makes everything seem better—including food. And on a rainy day, there is nothing more wonderful than the aroma of fresh bread baking in the oven.

The truth is, I never bake bread at home; I never have the time. And maybe that's the secret. When we're cruising, we do have the time, and both Taz and I spend many more hours in the galley being creative than we ever do when we're ashore. I've met a lot of other cruising couples who say the same thing: When they're on the boat they cook more, eat more, eat better . . . and never gain weight!

I think it's safe to say, then, that while the engine may be the heart of a cruising boat, the galley is definitely its soul. If the cook is happy, you can bet the rest of the crew will be happy, too.

LAYOUT

The galley deserves considerable thought and planning in the initial stages, before you ever leave the dock. Let's take a look at some of the components that contribute to a comfortable, workable galley.

Counter Space

I've said it before and I'll say it again: you cannot have enough counter space. Nothing is more frustrating than trying to cook a large meal with barely enough room to set down one bowl, let alone the bags of lettuce and tomatoes and the condiments you just pulled off the shelves. If you find you don't have enough space, some imagination plus a little carpentry can usually remedy the problem.

We have owned several boats that had covers for the stove—to extend the counter space. In practice, we found that we never used them because the times we needed extra space were also the times we needed the stove. We always ended up removing them. Wooden covers can be made into a chopping block or used to add a shelf somewhere else.

The space between a counter and a drawer or cabinet is usually "dead space." It can often be put to use by installing a pull-out cutting board that will do double-duty as extra counter space.

Another idea is to add a flip-up extension at the end of a counter. This might be something of a traffic hazard, but remember it's only up when you need it and will store flat against the bulkhead the rest of the time (Figure 3-1).

Sinks

Double sinks are great, provided at least one of them is large enough to hold a dinner plate and your largest cooking utensil. Many marine sinks are quite small—10 inches by 14 inches inside measurements are not uncommon. Consider that most dinner plates measure 10¼ inches diameter. You should be able to lay a plate down flat in the bottom of the sink. Even better, a 12-inch or 14-inch skillet should slide easily into the sink. If I had to make a choice, I would prefer one large sink to a pair of tiny ones. One side of a double sink can be fitted with a cutting board—a very handy arrangement (Figure 3-2). I also

FIGURE 3–1.   *This flip-up counter extension adds working space and folds flat against the end of the counter when not in use. Note the hook to hold it securely in the down position.*

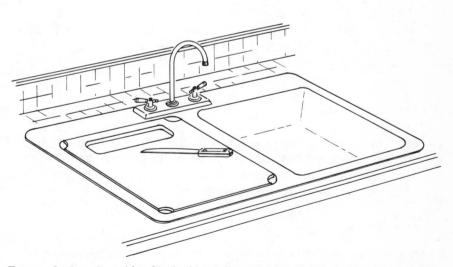

FIGURE 3–2.   *One side of a double sink can be fitted with a cutting board. The cutout provides a handle as well as an opening to catch scraps and drips.*

like a tall faucet, the ones sold for bar sinks are ideal. It makes it easier to fill up large pots and generally allows more working room, particularly if the sink is on the small side.

Ventilation

Ventilation is vitally important in the cruising galley. Opening ports, and a small opening hatch above the galley, are excellent for ventilation in good weather, but consider what happens if you're cooking pasta and a rain squall passes over. The ports and hatches must be closed and soon you and the boat are enveloped in a cloud of steam. It can become unbearable in a hurry, so there must be some means of extracting steam, smoke, and cooking odors, regardless of the weather.

Dorade vents are a good choice, and so is the installation of a low-profile exhaust vent in the top of a hatch. Nicro Marine's solar-powered exhaust vent is excellent for this application, since it requires no wiring. The newest version is equipped with a solar-charged battery so the fan will operate at night and on cloudy days.

Unfortunately, many galleys on powerboats are surrounded by fixed windows and located in a place where it is impossible to add natural ventilation. In this situation, an electrically driven exhaust fan is a must. Ideally, it would be placed over the stove. Ducting can be led behind overhead cabinets or through a bulkhead to exhaust to the outside. Simply installing a fan is not enough; all this will do is move the stale air through the rest of the boat. The air must be exhausted *out* of the cabin.

WATER SYSTEMS

Pressure water is the norm on all but the smallest boats. While I wouldn't consider *not* having a pressure system, I have to admit that it's a lot easier to waste water when all you have to do is turn on a faucet instead of pumping by hand.

Freshwater Pumps

Every cruising boat should have a manual pump in addition to the pressure system. Pressure water means an electric pump, subject to the same ills that can afflict every other electrical item aboard. If it's going to fail, you can bet it won't happen dockside, and you must be able to draw water without it. Adding a manual pump is not difficult, and it's not necessary to have one at every sink; usually just one in the galley will suffice. It can be either a hand pump, or a small faucet with a foot pump.

It's a good idea to add an accumulator tank, located between the pump and the first faucet (Figure 3-3). Since water is then drawn from the accumulator tank, it stops the rapid cycling of most pressure pumps, and extends the life of the pump as well as smoothing out the flow of water.

Saltwater Pumps

Saltwater pumps are a mixed blessing. Whether or not you want one depends on where you plan to cruise. When we were in the pristine waters of the Bahamas, we used saltwater constantly. Dishes and clothes were washed in it, followed by a freshwater rinse. For cooking, it was great for boiling eggs but too salty for pasta or rice so we would cut it by at least half with freshwater.

When we returned stateside we virtually stopped using saltwater, since there were very few harbors where the water was clean enough that I felt comfortable cooking or even washing dishes with it. As a result, the pump developed a horribly foul odor that required a complete disassembly and cleaning of the entire system to eradicate the smell. The experience convinced us not to install a saltwater pump on *Duchess*, although if we return to the islands for another lengthy cruise we may decide it's worth it after all.

Water Filters

You will find as you cruise that freshwater is not always as sweet and fresh as what you're used to at home. We have found "fresh" water so brackish you could taste the salt, water with an overwhelming sulfur smell and taste, and water that was brown with dirt particles. Don't assume that water is fresh just because a dock attendant says so. Taste it before it goes into the tanks; you may decide to hold off if possible. And when filling the tanks, be sure to use a hose that is

FIGURE 3–3.   *An accumulator tank stops the rapid cycling of pressure pumps and
smooths out the flow of the water.*

rated for drinking water. I use my own, not one that's been lying around on a fuel dock.

You'll also find that a water filter is a must when cruising, and there are several options to choose from. Pressure systems are generally installed with an in-line strainer between the tank and the pump, to prevent debris from entering and clogging the pump. You can take this one step further and install an additional strainer, like the ones sold for engine intake valves, to remove even greater amounts of dirt. These are strainers, however, not filters.

Most water filters are designed primarily to improve the taste of the water. A few will actually purify the water by removing bacteria and contaminants. The Seagull IV water purification system, made by General Ecology, is one of the best. It uses extreme microfiltration—down to 0.4 microns—to remove disease-causing bacteria, as well as removing a wide range of pollutants such as herbicides, pesticides, methylmercury, and chlorinated hydrocarbons. All filters use cartridges that must be changed periodically, and it's wise to carry enough cartridges to last the length of the cruise.

Since it makes sense to filter only water that will be consumed, not water used for washing and cleaning, it is common to install a separate hookup for the filtered water. Now if your system includes pressure water, a manual backup, and a saltwater pump, you could have as many as four faucets lined up behind the sink! If that seems a bit much, you might consider a unit like the Instapure filter, made by Teledyne Water Pik. It's a small unit that mounts directly on the faucet, with a selector switch to choose between filtered or unfiltered water. This unit, however, does not purify water, although it greatly improves the taste.

Water Heaters

Hot water is another convenience we take for granted ashore and have to plan for when cruising. A typical onboard heater has two ways of providing hot water. Underway, a heat exchanger uses waste heat from the engine's cooling water to heat the domestic supply. While dockside, or at anchor with the generator running, an electric heating element uses AC power to heat the water in the tank (Figure 3-4).

Demand-type water heaters, used extensively in Europe, are be-

FIGURE 3–4. *A typical hot water system. Water is heated underway by a heat exchanger, and dockside or at anchor by an electric heating element.*

coming more popular in this country. Rather than storing hot water inefficiently in a tank, water is heated instantly when the unit is activated, and only what is used is heated. The units that use propane, like the ones from Wolter Systems (which can also be used for cabin heat), are a good choice if that is also the cooking fuel. If these heaters are installed below, they must be vented to the outside, and the ones that do *not* require a pilot light are best for shipboard use.

Watermakers

Considering that powerboats usually have greater tankage given to fuel than to water, installing a watermaker (desalinator) may seem like a great idea (Figure 3-5). And it is, for a passagemaker, but less so for the coastal cruiser. Watermakers operate on the principle of reverse osmosis: seawater is forced, under pressure, through a semi-permeable membrane and the result is potable water (Figure 3-6). Simple enough, but the key word here is seawater. The membrane, designed for seawater (and in some cases, brackish water) will not hold up if used with the dirty water found in most harbors. Some of

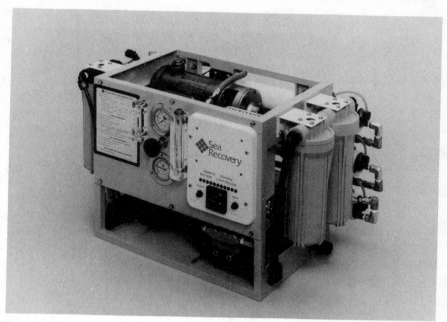

FIGURE 3–5. *Sea Recovery's Aqua Cube systems will produce up to 4 to 50 gallons per hour of clear drinking water. (Courtesy Sea Recovery Corporation)*

the larger, more sophisticated models have strainers, filters and oil/water separators, but the smaller units usually do not.

All watermakers must be used on a regular, almost daily, basis. If they are to sit idle for even a week, sometimes less, they must be thoroughly cleaned and treated with chemicals to inhibit bacteria growth.

Watermakers are available in a range of sizes, from small ones that produce less than two gallons an hour to monsters that will produce thousands of gallons in a day. If you decide to install a watermaker, think about how much water you really need, and what you will do with the excess. It makes no sense to dump half of it back over the side. Last year we were anchored for awhile next to some folks with a watermaker. We were envious of their long, luxurious showers, their great-tasting coffee, the daily freshwater washdown of their vintage Elco. And they were still producing such an excess that they invited everyone in the anchorage to row over with jugs and top up their tanks. While they were happy with their watermaker—pleased as punch, actually—they did admit that if their cruising was limited to

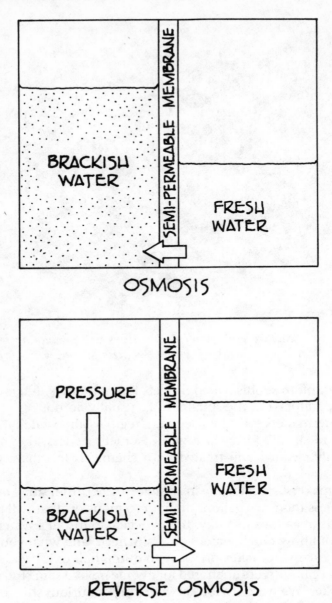

FIGURE 3–6. *Watermakers operate on the principle of reverse osmosis— seawater is forced, under pressure, through a semipermeable membrane, resulting in potable water.*

coastal areas where freshwater was easy to get, the watermaker would be more trouble than it was worth.

A final point about watermakers and water purifiers: This pure water tastes wonderful and contains nothing harmful. In fact, it contains nothing at all, so if it is the only water used for cooking and drinking, then you should add a vitamin/mineral supplement to your diet.

Conservation

Just about everyone who goes cruising becomes adept at conserving water. We quickly learn not to let the water run needlessly while brushing teeth, shaving or showering. Washing up a few lunch dishes does not require filling up a large sink when a mixing bowl filled with sudsy water will do fine. And while glass ports and windows, and varnished wood, do require wiping down with fresh water, sluicing mud from the anchor off the deck, and many other topside cleaning projects, can be done just as well with salt water.

STOVES

All stoves must be fitted with guard rails and clamps to hold pots securely (Figure 3-7). Don't think that because a powerboat doesn't heel that anything cooking on the stove is safe. It isn't. A powerboat is still a boat; it pitches and rolls and bounces around just like anything else that floats. That's why I think stoves installed fore and aft should be gimballed, although I have yet to see this done on a powerboat. Stoves located athwartships do not require gimballing.

Cooking utensils should be deep, and have tight-fitting lids. I never use a pressure cooker at home, but find it invaluable when cruising. It cooks up large batches of stew or spaghetti sauce quickly, tenderizes tough cuts of meat, and is a completely secure pot even without the pressure regulator.

Electric Stoves

Stove fuel is a matter of personal choice, although the norm on most powerboats is electricity. I dislike an all-electric galley for several

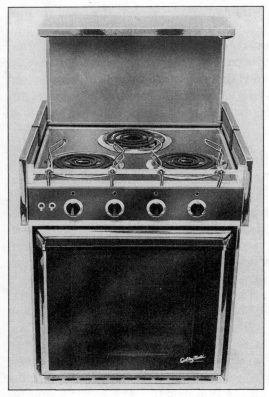

FIGURE 3–7.   *This electric stove from Galley Maid, with both sea rails and pot clamps, is well-equipped for cooking underway. (Courtesy Galley Maid Marine Products, Inc.)*

reasons. One is that I cook with gas at home and prefer it on the boat as well. But aside from that, an electric range in a house uses 220 current. While some marine ranges, like the ones from Galley Maid, can operate on either 110 or 220 current, only those that are hooked up for 220 will get as hot—and operate as efficiently—as the one at home. And I don't like having to run a generator every time I want to cook, especially for something as simple as a morning cup of coffee.

A great way to cut down on generator time (or save on fuel) is to fill a big thermos with hot water each morning. It will supply the crew with tea, coffee, or instant soups throughout the day, and it is particularly helpful when you're underway and don't want to spend extra time in the galley.

Propane Stoves

LPG (Liquefied Petroleum Gas—most commonly propane) is my choice for a galley fuel. Taz and I have installed it in every boat we've owned over the past twenty years, and would not use anything else. Propane burns clean and hot, it is cheap and available virtually anywhere, and used properly it is no more dangerous than other fuels, chemicals, and batteries found aboard.

Make no mistake, it *can* be dangerous. The gas is explosive, and it is heavier than air. If there is a leak the gas will not dissipate, it will sink to the bilge and wait for disaster to happen. There are any number of ways to prevent this, and most of them are based on common sense.

The tanks must be stowed topside, usually in their own vented box. They can go inside a deck locker, provided the compartment is fitted with a drain to carry any fumes overboard. I have seen several boats with tank storage incorporated into a stack. Tanks are available for either horizontal or vertical installation; and aluminum tanks are much better than steel ones, since they are lighter weight and do not rust.

The American Boat and Yacht Council (ABYC), which sets safety standards for the boating industry, says that fuel supply lines should be continuous lengths of tubing, piping, or hose. It makes sense—the fewer connections, the fewer chances of a leak. Copper tubing is frequently used, although flexible hose is often a better choice for a boat since it is not subject to corrosion and can be more easily routed around corners and through odd spaces without danger of kinking. Just be sure the hose used is rated for propane (a good source is an RV dealer) and that it is protected from chafe if it passes through a bulkhead.

One of the best safety features is a flame-failure device on all the burners. If the flame goes out for any reason, the gas is automatically shut off. This is fairly standard on quality stoves, and I wouldn't have a stove without it. While the best practice is to turn off the propane at the tank after each use, I know few people who always remember to do this. Therefore, it is essential to install a solenoid shutoff valve next to the stove. The control panels include a red light to remind the user that the stove is still on. Additionally, a gas detector can be installed, as low as possible in the boat, for further protection.

The system should be checked for leaks each time the tank is refilled and on a regular basis between fills—ABYC recommends at least every two weeks. Testing is not a difficult procedure. An LPG system should include a pressure regulator and a pressure gauge. To test, be sure the stove is off, and open the supply valve on the tank. Then turn the supply valve off and watch the pressure-gauge needle. The pressure should remain constant for at least fifteen minutes. If it drops, there is a leak, and all fittings and connections must be checked with a solution of soapy water to find the leak. If your installation does not have a pressure regulator, and some of them don't, then you should check the entire system with soapy water as a routine procedure.

CNG Stoves

CNG (Compressed Natural Gas) is a safer fuel than propane, but it has many disadvantages. It is lighter than air, so if there is a leak the gas will dissipate out hatches or ventilators—provided the hatches or vents are open. Because of this, the gas cylinders can be located just about anywhere. Some builders even put them below decks, and while this may be acceptable it still makes me nervous. Unlike propane, CNG is a high-pressure fuel, and I would feel like I was living with a bomb. Safety tests must be performed with a CNG system in the same manner as LPG.

CNG is both more costly and less efficient than propane. Filling a CNG cylinder can cost up to four times as much as filling a similar size propane tank. Manufacturers claim that one standard CNG cylinder will provide around twenty burning hours on one burner. That's not very much. On our last cruise, we were gone for six months and during that time cooked at least two meals a day, almost every day. We refilled a 20-pound propane tank *once*, at a cost of $6.00.

The real disadvantage of CNG comes when it is time to refill a cylinder, which happens frequently if you are cruising full-time. It is a federal regulation that the fuel distributor, not the boat owner, is the owner of the cylinder; so the cylinder must be returned to an authorized distributor for refilling. This can be a problem. Although distributors are more numerous than even five years ago, they are still few and far between. At Whittaker Creek Marina here in Oriental, the manager keeps a supply of filled cylinders for exchange, but this service is a rarity. More likely you will have to ship the cylinder yourself (UPS will handle gas cylinders) and then wait for it to be returned. It is the shipping costs, not the price of the gas itself, combined with the frequency of refilling, that makes this an expensive and inconvenient system.

CNG may be the ticket if your cruises are short and close to home, but if you are taking off for an extended time the hassle may not be worth it, and forget it if you are leaving U.S. waters. I personally feel that with a few common sense precautions, propane is a better choice than CNG or electricity; but again, that is only my opinion and this is a choice that boat owners must make for themselves.

Microwaves

While a microwave cannot replace the large oven on the stove, it can be a great addition to the galley as long as you have the power to run it (Figure 3-8). They are handy for quick snacks underway, and come

FIGURE 3-8.   *The very functional galley on the Krogen 42* Joan M *includes a microwave, mounted beneath an overhead cabinet, in addition to the range with oven. Note also the louvered cabinet doors that provide necessary ventilation.*

into their own on hot, sultry days when the last thing you want to do is turn on the stove and heat up the entire boat.

Barbecue Grills

Barbecue grills, of course, are the old standby for hot weather cruising. I like the ones that clamp on to a rail and extend outboard away from the boat, but whatever kind is used, care must be taken to locate it where a gust of wind will not blow cinders and smoke back aboard. If you have a barbecue that sits on the deck, it's a good idea to carry a fire-resistant rug, like the ones sold to go in front of a fireplace, to place beneath the grill and protect the deck. Skowhegan Moccasin, makers of footwear, also manufacture a flame-proof hibachi mat designed to be used aboard a boat. It can be hosed off, rolled up, and easily stowed after use. The barbecue should have its own storage bag (plastic-lined canvas is a good choice) so it can be put away without making a total mess of the locker.

REFRIGERATION

Refrigeration can cause more headaches than just about any other piece of equipment aboard, yet few of us would be willing to do without. I have cruised without it, and can now say with all honesty: whatever the price, it's worth it.

This is one area where powerboat cruisers could learn a few lessons from sailors. A refrigerator on a sailboat is almost always top-opening, partly to keep items intact when the boat heels, but also because it is the most efficient. Remember that heat rises, cold does not. When you open the door on a front-opening refrigerator, all the cold air spills out into the cabin. With a top-opening box, the cold air pretty much stays put.

Refrigeration is usually an option on a sailboat, so the box is built-in and can either be used for ice or a refrigeration unit can be installed, often at a remote location, depending on the type used. This means the box can be well-insulated right from the start and if it's not, it is seldom too difficult to add more. A powerboat, on the other hand, is likely to have a front-opening refrigerator that's right from either the RV market or a close relative. They are almost always poorly insulated. We chartered a boat last year with a 110-volt refrigerator that required running the generator a minimum of six hours a day to keep the ice cubes, and everything else in the freezer, frozen.

If you are running an air conditioner such an arrangement is no problem, but if you are after peace and quiet then it's another story. I don't know many folks who would consider ripping out a refrigerator and rebuilding the galley to install a different system, but if you are building a new boat give some thought to putting in a really efficient unit.

Efficiency starts with good insulation. Polyurethane foam works the best. It is a closed-cell foam, and is around 30 percent more efficient than Styrofoam, which is "open-celled." The insulation should be a minimum of four inches thick, and this includes the door. The more insulation the better, although you can reach a point of diminishing returns where the box is so small it is useless. Adding insulation to an existing unit is usually not that difficult as long as it's a built-in box and you can get inside the surrounding cabinets, but that still leaves the door with minimal insulation.

Most modern marine refrigerators are either copper or black. Why, I don't know. If they are placed where the sun is beating down through a large window all day, then either paint the door white or cover it with white formica, and put a curtain over the window. You'll be amazed at the difference it will make in running time. Large upright models should have separate doors for the freezer and refrigerator sections. And try to train the crew to think about what they want *before* they open the door. Studying the contents of an open refrigerator the way we do at home is a definite no-no aboard ship.

Most powerboats have a dual voltage, AC/DC system, since they generally have ample battery capacity for operation at anchor or without the generator, and can run off AC power dockside and 12-volt underway. A straight AC refrigerator is not a good idea, even if you do run a generator a lot for other systems. With dual voltage, you won't lose a freezer full of food if the generator decides to pack it in for a while. A single-voltage DC unit is fine, however, since the batteries will be charged underway or through the converter when dockside or when running the generator.

Another alternative would be to install an inverter to take care of an AC refrigerator when the generator is not running. See the chapter on electricity for a closer look at using an inverter for this, and other, purposes.

Hold-over systems use a compressor to cool-down holding plates located within the refrigerator. Installed in custom-made boxes, they are efficient but they do require an engine running on a regular basis, usually an hour a day although a really efficient system can go for two days (except in the tropics). The biggest disadvantage is that you become a slave to the system. The engine must be run even if the boat is dockside, and if you want to leave the boat and fly home for a week you must either get someone to "baby-sit" or completely empty the refrigerator. Most of us do choose a dock if we are leaving the boat for a while, and it just makes sense to be able to have the refrigerator running off shore power while we're gone.

STOWAGE

If there's one rule about galley stowage, it has to be this: keep it dry. In the damp atmosphere aboard a boat, dry foodstuffs can become lumpy and moldy, fresh fruit and vegetables will rot, and metal utensils rust or corrode.

Unless cans are stowed in the bilge, we have never found it necessary to varnish them. The paper labels can come off, however, so it's a good idea to write the contents on the top of the can with a permanent maker (a laundry marker works well).

Flour, sugar, rice, cereals—anything that must stay dry—should be removed from its original wrapping and placed in either a glass or plastic container with a tight-fitting lid. Glass is the best, but it is breakable. Cut out any instructions and place them in the container as well. To prevent weevils, I also add a whole bay leaf to each one.

There's another good reason for getting rid of all paper and cardboard wrappers. Cockroaches will lay their eggs in the folds of bags and boxes, and the babies will feed on the glue when they hatch. This is seldom a problem ashore because we buy cereal and such one box at a time. When we stock up for a cruise, we may buy a case of our favorite cereal, and it's this long-term storage that invites the little devils to set up house. (See Chapter 5 for ways to deal with pests aboard.)

Dividing large shelves into smaller compartments will keep things from sliding around underway and it will almost double the storage space. Narrow strips of thin plywood can be used for permanent divisions (Figure 3-9). My preference is to use plastic baskets and trays. These are available at most hardware or discount stores (like K Mart) in such an infinite variety of shapes and sizes that I've always been able to mix and match for a perfect fit.

All cabinets will benefit from ventilation, but it is especially important in lockers where fresh produce is stored. Solid cabinet doors can be modified with inserts of louvers or caning, or by drilling ventilation holes or making cutouts in a pleasing pattern (Figure 3-10). I saw a great idea on a boat that was heading for Europe. The owner cut out the bottom of one shelf and replaced it with window screen, so air could circulate all around the vegetables stored there

FIGURE 3–9.   *The galley shelves above the refrigerator on the 64-foot Consolidated Commuter,* Ragtime, *are divided into numerous compartments. It helps keep everything in place and increases the amount of usable storage space.*

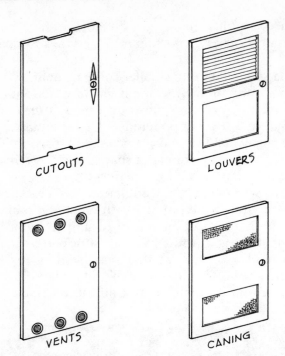

FIGURE 3—10.   *Solid cabinet doors can usually be modified to increase the ventilation to the lockers. This is particularly important for food lockers.*

(Figure 3-11). Fruits and vegetables are also happy kept in nets or baskets hung from the overhead or under soffet cabinets.

On most cruising boats, every available inch of bulkhead space in the galley is eventually covered, and with good reason. It's handy to have frequently used items within easy reach, especially small ones that can get lost in the jumble of a drawer. Hooks can hold bottle openers, ice picks, oven mitts, can openers, spatulas, and wooden spoons. Spice racks, knife racks, glass holders, shelves for condiments, all can free up cabinet space for larger items. Hooks underneath overhead cabinets can hold coffee cups or mugs. To keep them from clanking together when underway, mount the hooks so the cups "nest" inside each other—they will swing as a unit and never make a sound (this only works for cups, not for straight-sided mugs).

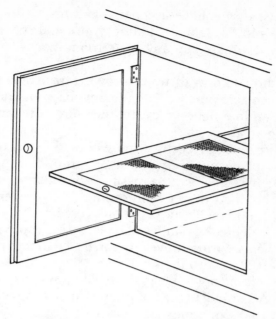

FIGURE 3–11. *Replacing the bottom of a shelf with window screen will create an ideal place to store fresh vegetables.*

GARBAGE

It's not anyone's favorite topic of conversation, but it is something that must be dealt with on a daily basis, and the trash can pile up in a hurry on a cruising boat. Anything smaller than a standard kitchen-size garbage bin will be useless in a galley. Where to put it is the challenge. Sometimes there is room underneath the galley sink, although you may have to remove a shelf to fit it in. In L-shaped or U-shaped galleys, that inaccessible corner can hold a large trash can by making a cutout with a removable cover in the countertop. If the galley is next to a companionway, a trash bin may fit behind the ladder. Wherever it goes, it must have a secure lid to contain odors and keep the contents from spilling if it gets knocked over.

I have long believed that trash compactors were really designed for cruising boats. If you have a generator, a trash compactor could easily be the most valuable addition you could make to the galley, and they don't take up any more room than a large trash can would.

As we all should know by now, throwing trash over the side is no longer an acceptable practice. What many may not know is that, as the result of an international treaty, there are now laws governing the dumping of trash at sea. You must be at least twelve miles offshore before you can legally dispose of food, paper bags, glass, or metal cans that have not been ground up (ground trash must be able to pass through a screen with a mesh of 25mm or smaller).

No plastic products of any kind can be thrown over the side, no matter where you are. Plastic is not biodegradable. Styrofoam cups, for example, will break up into small pieces, but those pieces last for hundreds of years. Virtually every ocean beach in the world now has Styrofoam mixed in with the sand.

Not only is plastic not biodegradable, but it is a major killer of fish and wildlife. According to the National Wildlife Federation, a million seabirds and 10,000 marine mammals are killed each year by entanglement with plastic trash including fishing lines and netting, plastic bags, six-pack rings, and strapping bands. Another report, from the National Marine Fisheries Service, gives a different number. Their report says that around 30,000 northern fur seals die each year from netting alone.

Sea turtles mistake floating plastic for one of their favorite foods—jellyfish—and the result is a slow and painful death. Turtles, seabirds, fish, and mammals, all can be ensnared and killed by the plastic rings from six-pack cartons, monofilament fishing lines—any kind of plastic. It behooves us all to go beyond simply not tossing plastic overboard and try to cut down on using plastic products as much as possible.

Prevention is always the best policy, and the less trash you create the fewer problems you will have. Repackaging stores into airtight containers keeps them dry and bug-free, and it also gets rid of a tremendous amount of trash before you ever leave the dock. If you must buy drinks with six-pack rings, be sure to cut the rings apart before throwing them away, even though you are disposing of your trash ashore. And while paper plates and cups may cut down a bit on dishwashing, they will fill up a garbage can in a hurry. With a little imagination, good meals can be created out of leftovers so food is consumed, not thrown away.

A large part of the joy of cruising lies in our close association with nature and all her beauty, and it is up to each of us, as individuals, to make sure she remains beautiful. No government regulations will accomplish it. We must accept the responsibility ourselves.

CHAPTER 4

Electricity

GONE ARE THE DAYS when cruising in a powerboat meant traveling from marina to marina, primarily so the boat could be plugged into shore power and the good life could continue—just like home. But just because we have discovered the joys of anchoring out doesn't mean we must give up the good life and all the amenities that electricity can provide, not by a long shot. Smaller and smaller boats are being equipped with generators, and a generator is frequently standard equipment on larger boats. Generators are great and can indeed make life aboard as comfortable as ashore, but they are not the only way of obtaining electricity. There are other options available and you may find that some of them are simpler, more economical, and better suited to your particular purposes than a generator.

ALTERNATING CURRENT (AC) SYSTEMS

Most boats have either a 30 amp or 50 amp 110-volt electrical system, with 30 amp being the most common. Figure 4-1 shows a diagram of a typical single phase 110 system. Large yachts may use a 50 amp 220-volt system for greater power. To understand what this means, we use the formula *volts × amps = watts*. 110 volts × 30 amps = 3,300 watts of available power. A 50 amp 110-volt system gives an increase to 5,500 watts. If you were to add up the wattage requirements of every piece of gear aboard, you would probably find that the total far exceeds this available power, but it would be rare that you would ever turn on everything at once. On the other hand, if you frequently trip a circuit breaker because the air conditioner is running, the refrigerator kicks in, and then someone flips on the television or a toaster and everything comes to a screeching halt, you need to think about upgrading to a more powerful system or training the crew to be more aware of who is running what at any given time.

The electrical current, from whatever source (shoreside or onboard system), goes to the electrical panel (Figure 4-2) through a main circuit breaker and is distributed from there to smaller, or branch, circuits that provide electricity for outlets or appliances throughout the boat. Each branch circuit must be provided with its own individual circuit breaker. And circuit breakers, not fuses, are the only way to go aboard a cruising boat.

A circuit breaker does two things when it stops the flow of current: It prevents shock from a short circuit and prevents electrical fire from heat buildup. So even though the most likely cause of a tripped circuit breaker is simply an overload, it could be an indication of something more serious and both the system and any appliances that were plugged in at the time should be checked thoroughly before the breaker is reset and you forget about it.

Even though every boat will have a different electrical system (and the older the boat, the more "different" the systems can be), the basic principles remain the same. When an appliance is turned on, current travels from the electrical source to the appliance through an ungrounded conductor—the hot wire. The hot wire is either red or black, and is totally insulated from ground. When the appliance is turned off, the current returns to the source through a grounded conductor. This wire is called the neutral conductor and it is always white. A third wire, called the ground wire or grounding conductor, does not carry current but is there to protect people from shock and equipment from damage. The ground wire is always green.

Ground-fault shock is one of the most frequent, and lethal, elec-

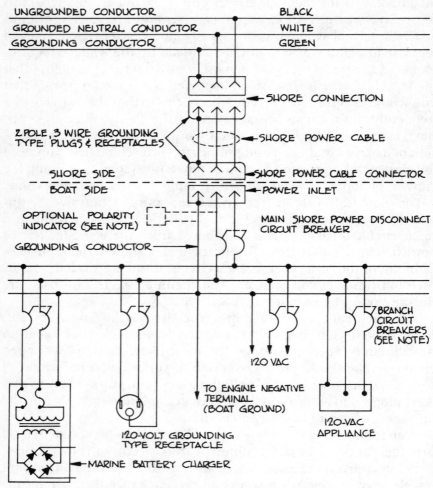

UNGROUNDED CONDUCTOR   BLACK
GROUNDED NEUTRAL CONDUCTOR   WHITE
GROUNDING CONDUCTOR   GREEN

◄ SHORE CONNECTION

2 POLE, 3 WIRE GROUNDING
TYPE PLUGS & RECEPTACLES   ◄ SHORE POWER CABLE

SHORE SIDE   SHORE POWER CABLE CONNECTOR
BOAT SIDE   POWER INLET

OPTIONAL POLARITY   MAIN SHORE POWER DISCONNECT
INDICATOR (SEE NOTE)   CIRCUIT BREAKER

GROUNDING CONDUCTOR

BRANCH
CIRCUIT
BREAKERS
(SEE NOTE)

120 VAC

TO ENGINE NEGATIVE
TERMINAL
(BOAT GROUND)

120-VOLT GROUNDING   120-VAC
TYPE RECEPTACLE   APPLIANCE

MARINE BATTERY CHARGER

NOTE : SINGLE-POLE BRANCH CIRCUIT BREAKERS (IN UNGROUNDED
        CONDUCTOR) MAY BE USED IF POLARITY INDICATOR IS USED

FIGURE 4–1.   *Single-phase 120-volt system with shore-grounded neutral conductor and grounding conductor. (Courtesy the American Boat & Yacht Council's 1985 E-8 from "Standards and Recommended Practices for Small Craft.")*

FIGURE 4–2. *The electrical panel is typically divided into AC and DC sections. Note the small lights around the perimeter to make it easy to use at night.*

trical accidents, particularly on or around a boat. A ground fault is a failure in a circuit that allows current to flow from a hot wire to ground. Common causes are old, faulty electrical tools and wiring that has been damaged by moisture or frayed insulation.

Ground fault protection (GFP) breakers will protect circuits and gear, but a ground fault circuit interrupter (GFCI) is the only thing that will protect *people* (Figure 4-3). Based on American Boat and Yacht Council (ABYC) recommendations, new boats should now have GFCI's installed on all AC receptacles located in the galley, head, machinery area or on a weather deck. However, you're not likely to find GFCI's on an older boat, and adding them is undoubtedly one of the best moves you can make to ensure the safety of you and your crew. And—good news—they are quite inexpensive. Hubbell's GFCI receptacle, for instance, retails for about $26.00. Rather than install one at each receptacle, you can put one at the first receptacle from the electrical panel on each branch circuit, and it will protect each receptacle on that circuit. It's cheap insurance.

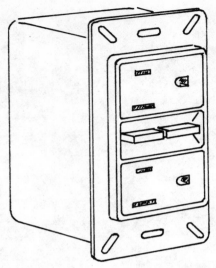

FIGURE 4–3. *A ground-fault circuit interrupter (GFCI) receptacle should be installed in the galley, head, machinery area or on a weather deck.*

Figuring Power Requirements

How much electrical power do you need? If you're like most of us, probably a bunch. I always think of cruising as getting back to "the simple life," and in many ways it is, but there are quite a few conveniences that I don't want to give up; and the older I get, the more adamant I am about not giving them up.

Boatbuilders have recognized this as a common trait, and a new boat is likely to have an adequate AC system, or at least offer it as an option. Older boats are more likely to adhere to the simple life principle with woefully skimpy wiring. And since we all like to add more from time to time, what is adequate today may not be tomorrow. Whether you have an old boat or a new one, it's a good idea to sit down and work through a load calculation to find out just what the boat can handle, especially before you run out to buy more equipment that you feel is necessary for a happy cruise.

The following calculations are from the American Boat and Yacht Council's 1985 "Standards and Recommended Practices for Small Craft," and will give you a very good idea of your AC power requirements. To find amperes for equipment rated in watts, use the following formula:

watts divided by volts = amperes

a. Lighting Fixtures and Receptacles—Length times width of living space (excluding spaces exclusively for machinery and open deck areas) times 2 watts per square foot.

Formula: Length × width × 2 = _____ lighting watts.

b. Small Appliances—Galley and Dinette Areas—Number of circuits times 1,500 watts for each 20 ampere appliance receptacle circuit.

Formula: Number of Circuits × 1,500 = _____ small appliance watts.

c. Total

Formula: Lighting watts plus small appliance watts = _____ total watts.

d. Load Factor

Formula: First 2,000 total watts at 100% = _____

Remaining total watts times 35% = _____

Total watts divided by system voltage = _____ amperes.

e. If shore power system is to operate on 240 volts, split and balance loads into Leg A and Leg B. If shore power system is to operate on 120 volts, use Leg A only.

	Leg A	Leg B
Total amperes from "d" above	_____	_____

f. Add nameplate amperes for motor and heater loads:

	Leg A	Leg B
Exhaust and supply fans	_____	_____
Air conditioners*,**	_____	_____
Electric, gas or oil heaters*	_____	_____
25% of largest motor in above items	_____	_____
Sub-Total	_____	_____

Note: * Omit smaller of these two, except include any motor common to both functions.

** If system consists of 3 or more independent units, adjust the total by multiplying by 75% diversity factor.

g. Add nameplate amperes at indicated use factor percentage for:

	LEG A	LEG B
Disposal—10%	_____	_____
Water Heater—100%	_____	_____
Wall-mounted Ovens—75%	_____	_____
Cooking Units—75%	_____	_____
Refrigerator—100%	_____	_____
Freezer—100%	_____	_____
Ice Maker—50%	_____	_____
Dishwasher—25%	_____	_____
Washing Machine—25%	_____	_____
Dryer—25%	_____	_____
Trash Compactor—10%	_____	_____
Air Compressor—10%	_____	_____
Battery Chargers—100%	_____	_____
Vacuum System—10%	_____	_____
Other Fixed Appliances	_____	_____
	_____	_____
	_____	_____
	_____	_____
Sub-Total	_____	_____
**Adjusted Sub-Total	_____	_____

Note: ** If four or more appliances are installed, adjust the total by multiplying by 60% diversity factor.

h. Add amperes for free-standing range as distinguished from separate oven and cooking units as provided for in "g" above. Derive from following table by dividing watts by 120 volts or 240 volts depending on which unit is installed.

Nameplate Rating (watts)	Use (watts)
10,000 or less	80% of rating
10,001—12,500	8,000
12,501—13,500	8,400
13,501—14,500	8,800
14,501—15,500	9,200
15,501—16,500	9,600
16,501—17,500	10,000

Sub-Total _____ _____

	Leg A	Leg B
i. Lighting and small appliances "e"	_____	_____
Motors "f"	_____	_____
Fixed Appliances "g"	_____	_____
Free-Standing Range "h"	_____	_____
Total	_____	_____

Note: If the totals for Legs A and B are unequal, use the larger value to determine the total power required.

The total may surprise you. If it seems excessively high, you might think about changing some of your equipment (like the refrigerator) to 12-volt instead of 110, replacing an electric stove with propane, or as gear wears out, choosing a replacement that's more energy-conscious. Quite a few items that we think of as 110 are actually 12-volt, and have an internal transformer that allows them to be plugged into an ordinary household outlet. Most computers, for example, are really 12-volt, and a knowledgeable technician can make the switch. Many cruisers find, however, that they use less power at anchor than dockside. In a crowded marina, for instance, it may be necessary to run the air conditioner night and day. But at anchor, where there's almost always a cooling breeze, just opening ports or running a small fan may be all that's needed. And those who are lucky enough to have a washer and dryer aboard generally use them only when dockside, both for the electricity available and to be sure of an ample water supply without depleting the boat's tankage.

Shore Power

All ship-to-shore power cords should be of marine quality, with a heavy vinyl cover that protects the twist-lock plug and connector. The boat's power inlet should have a screw-type waterproof cover. Hubbell and Marinco are two of the most popular manufacturers of quality marine electrical equipment.

Obviously the shore power system must be rated high enough to handle the load. If you've done the load calculations and find that the total is too high for a single cord, you may have to split the system and balance the load between two power cords (Figure 4-4). A common arrangement is to have one 30-amp system for lighting and appliances, and a separate 30-amp system dedicated solely to an air conditioner.

A fact of life when cruising is that the electrical outlets at marinas are far from standard. Sooner or later you will need an adapter to

FIGURE 4–4.   *This shore-power receptacle can be used with either one or two power cords to supply the boat with 110, or 220, electricity. (Photo by Jill Lorenz)*

plug in your cord dockside. It's a good idea to make up at least one or two—generally one that will allow you to step down, from 50 to 30, or 30 to 15—before leaving for a cruise. Some marinas have "loaners," but chances are high that they will be in use when you get there and there's no guarantee that you will be able to purchase one on the spot. Remember that when you step down to a lower amperage you must adjust your power usage accordingly.

If you cruise in the boondocks, you will sometimes find a marina with nothing more sophisticated than a receptacle for a household-type extension cord. You can make up an adapter for this possibility, but be very careful about plugging in. Such receptacles are an indication that the wiring is old and probably none too safe. You are really better off not plugging in at all but just relying entirely on the ship's onboard power system.

A boat's AC system is polarized; that is, all wiring connections are made in the same way to ensure that electrical current always flows in the same direction in each circuit. Wires are color-coded so you know which is which. Reverse polarity can cause all sorts of havoc.

If the hot (red or black) and neutral (white) wires are reversed, it can cause damage to equipment and deliver an electrical shock to the crew.

If the neutral (white) and ground (green) wires are reversed, electrolytic corrosion is the result. Hooking up to a dockside receptacle with reversed polarity will start an attack on the boat's metal fittings that are below the waterline. Saltwater is a great conductor of stray current. Actually, the dockside receptacle may be wired correctly, but if another boat with reverse polarity plugs into the same circuit you are on, your polarity will be reversed as well.

That's why it's so important to always check the polarity when you pull into a new marina. Many electrical panels are now fitted with reverse polarity warning lights. If yours is not, buy a circuit tester that can be plugged into an outlet, similar to the one shown in Figure 4-5. This tester will check both hot and neutral wires for reverse polarity, check for reversal of hot and ground wires, as well as check for an open ground wire.

Another form of protection is the installation of an isolation transformer. These are very common on steel and aluminum boats. An isolation transformer establishes the polarity aboard the boat by isolating the ship's electrical system from shore ground—the power

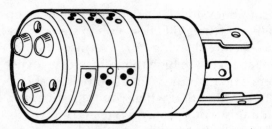

FIGURE 4—5.   *Marinco's 9030 circuit tester for 30-amp 125-volt locking recepta-cles will check hot and neutral wires for reverse polarity, check for reversal of hot and ground wires, and check for an open ground wire.* (*Courtesy Marinco Electrical Products*)

is transferred magnetically, so the boat is protected from any electrolytic corrosion caused by stray current.

Generators

On a powerboat that is all-electric (air conditioner, refrigerator, range, microwave, etc.), a generator is just about a necessity when the boat is used for cruising (Figure 4-6). Check your load calculations and be sure the generator is large enough to handle your lifestyle.

Both gasoline and diesel generators are available, and it makes sense to have one that uses the same fuel as the main engines. Most permanently mounted generators are water-cooled, and require the same service and attention as the boat's engines. They are also just as noisy as the main engines, which is their major drawback at anchor. You can purchase soundproof enclosures designed specifically for generators. A soundproof enclosure, along with a good muffler for the exhaust, will make you a better neighbor in the anchorage as well as make life easier (quieter) aboard your own boat.

A remote start-up switch is a must. Or you can install an automatic start-stop control that will automatically start the generator whenever an appliance is turned on or plugged in and stop the generator when the load ceases.

Inverters

A solid-state inverter converts 12-volt DC current to 110-volt AC power (Figure 4-7). Some of the larger models will operate from a

FIGURE 4–6.   *A generator is just about a necessity on a cruising boat that is ''all-electric.''* (*Photo by Jill Lorenz*)

24- or 32-volt DC system. They can be wired to draw current from either the ship's batteries or the engine alternator, although directly from the battery is the most common arrangement.

An inverter can greatly reduce generator-running time, and in many instances eliminate the need for a generator entirely. If you frequently use an air conditioner or a watermaker, and cook with an electric range, then you definitely need a generator. According to Dytek Laboratories, it is not cost effective to run appliances with high-wattage loads such as clothes dryers, air conditioners, water heaters, or electric stoves, with an inverter. But for most other applications an inverter will perform just as well as a generator, and it will do it silently. If you are using the generator primarily for refrigeration, then an inverter is a better choice. A refrigerator only runs for about 20 minutes out of every hour during the day, and less at night, yet if you are running a generator you are burning fuel continuously regardless of the load, and running for many hours at idle for low-wattage output increases maintenance and shortens the life of the generator.

FIGURE 4–7.   *An inverter, like this 2012 model from Trace, converts DC current (usually from the ship's batteries) to 110-volt AC power. (Courtesy Trace Engineering)*

One of the best features of an inverter is that they are noiseless. With an inverter, rather than starting off the morning by firing up the generator, you can plug in an electric coffee maker, make toast, or pop something into the microwave, and still enjoy the peace and quiet of the anchorage.

Be sure the inverter you choose has surge capacity, particularly if you are using it for a refrigerator. Most motors produce a start-up surge for a few seconds that can be several times higher than their rated wattage. Heart Interface's 1200-watt inverter, for instance, will handle a brief surge of up to 6000 watts.

Some of the newer inverters will also function as a battery charger (Trace offers this as a "Standby Option" for all of their models.) This is a nice feature since it combines two pieces of equipment into one. Most of them will sense when AC power is available to charge the batteries, and will automatically return to the inverter mode when the AC power is shut down.

Inverters do generate heat when they are operating, and should be installed in a well-ventilated space—not the engine room. Inverters are made with standard outlets so appliances can be plugged in directly to them, but most of them can also be wired into the ship's AC system. It's a good practice to install the inverter with its own circuit breaker and wire it only to specific outlets. If you wire it so it will supply power to the entire AC system, it is essential to also install a switch so power can be delivered from only *one* source at a time—either shore power, the generator, or the inverter.

How much power an inverter can actually deliver, and for how long, will depend greatly on the state of your batteries. We'll talk about batteries in detail in the next section, but I would like to point out here that an inverter should be only operated with deep-cycle batteries, and never with the engine-starting battery. A good quality inverter will include an automatic shutoff in case of an overload or a short circuit, or if the batteries get too low. The chart in Table 4-1 shows how many amp-hours will be used for some typical appliances.

AC Alternators

Another source for AC power is from a 110-volt AC alternator belted to the main engine. Two types are available—one that is installed in

Table 4-1
Approximate Amp-Hours Consumed by Typical Appliances in Daily Use

Appliance	Watts	Daily Minutes of Use	AMP/Hours Used from 12-Volt Battery
Color TV	100	120	18.0
Blender	300	5	2.0
Food Processor	400	6	3.3
Shaver	10	12	0.2
Water Pic	90	3	0.4
Hair Dryer	1200	12	20.0
VCR	60	120	10.0
Microwave	850	18	21.3
Toaster	1000	5	7.6
Coffee Maker	1200	10	16.7
Refrigerator	500	480	33.0

addition to the 12-volt alternator, and another that can replace it. This second type has two sets of windings that can produce either 12-volt or 110-volt power.

The big disadvantage of AC alternators is that they only work when the engine is running. You will have plenty of power underway, but at anchor you must run the engine (just like running a generator) if you want 110-volt electricity.

Newer models are built to deliver a steady supply of 110-volt 60-cycle current, regardless of the engine speed. Some of the older ones depended on engine rpm's to ensure 60 cycles which would make them pretty useless on today's high-speed powerboats.

DIRECT CURRENT (DC) SYSTEMS

It's amazing how many 12-volt appliances are now available. Some of them are ideal for use on boats and some of them aren't. Converting to 12-volt seems to work best with low-wattage equipment. *Duchess's* 12-volt system includes all her lighting, a color TV, the refrigerator/freezer, several fans, pumps, a vacuum cleaner, and of course all electronics. Everything performs perfectly, except for the vacuum cleaner, which is nothing if not anemic. A vacuum cleaner is a high-wattage appliance, and the 12-volt ones never seem to have the power of one that runs off AC.

Other interesting items that have come on the market recently include 12-volt blenders, microwaves, and toasters. I haven't tried any of them, but judging from their wattage I would say probably yes to a blender (300–400 watts), maybe to a microwave (600–800 watts), and no to a toaster (1000–1500 watts). How well anything performs is directly related to the condition of the ship's batteries, so let's take a close look at them.

The Marine Battery

Batteries used aboard ship are of two basic types—an automotive battery similar to the one in your car, used for a starting battery; and a marine deep-cycle battery, used as the "house" battery. Most powerboats have one or two starting batteries, and one or more separate banks of deep-cycle batteries that handle all the rest of the 12-volt or 24-volt demands (Figure 4-8).

FIGURE 4—8.   *A deep-cycle battery is built to handle the continuous, but usually low-load, demands of day-to-day cruising.* (*Photo courtesy of Surrette America*)

It's important to understand the difference. Automotive batteries are built to deliver the high-amp requirements of starting an engine—and it's particularly high with a diesel—then the alternator takes over to supply electricity and recharge the battery. An automotive battery cannot handle the slow but steady discharge imposed by lighting, pumps, radios and other DC equipment found on the average cruising boat. Try to use an automotive battery in this way and after 30 or so of these "deep" discharges and recharges the battery will be completely dead.

Marine deep-cycle batteries, with their thick, heavy plates, are built to handle the continuous but generally low-load demands of day-to-day life aboard ship. Deep-cycle batteries are always big and heavy. Rolls Marine's 220-amp hour battery weighs a hefty 164 pounds. Weight is a good indication of a battery that will give quality service for many years.

When we think of a 12-volt system most of us naturally think of installing 12-volt batteries, but that is not the only way to go. Two 6-volt batteries wired in series to produce 12 volts will store greater amp-hours than one 12-volt battery, and take up less space (they are smaller in width and depth, but greater in height). They are also usually heavier-duty; that is, they have thicker plates, and should therefore outlast a 12-volt battery.

Battery Care and Storage

When a battery is being charged, hydrogen and oxygen gases are formed. As the battery reaches full charge, and especially if the battery is overcharged, these gases create an extremely explosive mixture. It is essential that batteries are stored in a dry, well-ventilated area and away from any appliance that could cause a spark and blow your boat (and possibly you as well) to smithereens. The storage area should also be one with easy access—if you can get to the batteries without moving a ton of gear, you're a lot more likely to give them the routine maintenance they deserve. And each battery should be placed in its own lead- or fiberglass-lined box, and the box well-secured to keep the batteries from shifting or turning over in rough seas.

The liquid in the battery's cells is electrolyte, a mixture of sulfuric acid and distilled water. If you've ever spilled battery acid on your clothes, you know how fast it can destroy fabric, to say nothing of what it can do to your skin. If you get any on you, wash immediately with water and baking soda to neutralize the acid.

The batteries should be checked on a weekly basis when you are cruising, or even more frequently if you are putting in a lot of running time. Check the electrolyte level of each cell, and add distilled water if necessary. If the battery seems to be drinking an awful lot of water, or if one cell is always low, it is a sure sign that the battery is going bad.

The best way to keep tabs on the health of your batteries and their state of charge is by measuring the specific gravity of the electrolyte with a hydrometer (Figure 4-9). Since the hydrometer is calibrated to give the specific gravity at 80 degrees F., an adjustment will have to be made—a chart is generally included with the hydrometer. At 1.265, the battery is fully charged; lower readings indicate less than full charge.

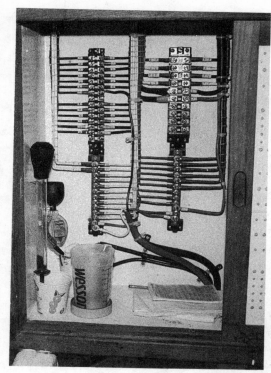

FIGURE 4–9. *This sliding-door cabinet, located next to the banks of batteries, provides access to the back of an electrical panel as well as a home for two hydrometers. One is mounted securely in brackets on the left side of the cabinet.*

Another way to monitor the battery's state of charge is with a voltmeter, preferably one with a scale that reads between 10 and 15 volts dc, in tenth-volt increments. The Guest Company makes a solid-state voltage scanner that will monitor up to four banks of batteries as well as showing if the battery charger and alternator are performing correctly.

Keeping the batteries dry and clean is just as important as monitoring the charge rate. The slightest amount of corrosion can cause stray currents that rob the battery's power. Clean the top of the battery, using water and baking soda if there is any sign of acid, and make sure that all connections and terminals are shiny bright and clean.

Battery-Charging Sources

An inexpensive automotive battery charger has no place on a cruising boat—only one designed specifically for the marine environment should be used. A marine battery charger, often called a converter

(Figure 4-10), uses a transformer to isolate the AC shore power from the ship's DC system. The connection is magnetic, not electrical, so the problems caused by stray current are avoided. A marine charger is also almost always automatic—it will shut itself off when the batteries are fully charged, and on again when it senses a drain.

According to Raritan Engineering Company (manufacturers of Crown automatic converters), a converter should be installed in a dry area and as close to the batteries as possible. It's best not to install one in the engine room; but wherever it goes, be sure it receives enough ventilation to dissipate the heat generated when it is operating.

Powerboats are usually equipped with large enough alternators that there is seldom a problem keeping the batteries topped up as long as passages are being made. At anchor, those with independent

FIGURE 4—10.   *A marine battery charger uses a transformer to isolate the AC shore power from the ship's DC system. The connection is magnetic, not electrical. (Courtesy Raritan Engineering Company, Inc.)*

generators can charge batteries whenever the generator is running. It's the rest of us—those without a generator—that must run the ship's engine on a regular basis if we choose to anchor out for more than a few days. I've always hated having to do this, partly because of the noise and also because it seemed like a waste of fuel, plus engines aren't happy being run for long periods at slow speeds out of gear.

There are a couple of alternative energy sources worth exploring. I know they won't begin to handle the load of most powerboats, but for some they can offer a real boost. Consider, too, that as the world energy problems grow, several things are happening. The fuel we burn to power our boats and run all our equipment is becoming scarce and more expensive. Remember the energy crisis? It not only can happen again, it most probably will. Along with this, however, technology is making strides in alternative energy sources. Anchorages are full of sailboats sporting solar panels and wind generators, and if you think all they are powering with them are a few lights and a small radio, you couldn't be more wrong.

Solar panels in particular have always seemed to me to be ideally suited for powerboats (Figure 4-11). Powerboat decks and cabin tops are generally clear and uncluttered compared to most sailboats, and they don't have the mass of rigging and sails to cast shadows everywhere. The top of the pilot house on *Duchess* will soon be covered with an array of solar panels. Although they are expensive, the prices get lower each year as the quality of the cells and their mountings goes up.

Of course, how well solar cells work has a lot to do with where they are mounted. On a boat swinging at anchor, it is impossible to keep the panels at the proper south-facing angle, so you can never count on them delivering their maximum-rated wattage. Still, we have had great success with them—although, as I mentioned before, our electrical requirements are lower than most.

An excellent application for solar power is to use it for individual items. *Duchess* has three of Nicro/Marine's Day/Night solar exhaust ventilators that include a ni-cad battery for operation at night (see The Comfort Factor chapter for a detailed discussion).

Wind generators provide greater power for less money than solar panels, but their use on powerboats is not always practical. With no rigging to hoist them aloft, they would almost certainly require a permanent mount—one that was high enough for the blades to clear

FIGURE 4–11.   *These solar-charge controllers will control the rate of charge to the batteries from solar panels. The C-30/A model includes an automatic nighttime disconnect. (Courtesy Trace Engineering)*

all obstructions, including the crew, and only the big ones produce enough electricity to make them worthwhile.

Load Calculations

Just like the load calculations for the AC system, it's a good idea to do one for your DC system. Your batteries may be perfectly adequate now, but as you add goodies for cruising they may not be, and it will help if you know what your base is. The worksheet on pages 102–103, taken from the ABYC Standards, will help you decide if your battery supply is ample or if you need to think about upgrading before you take off.

ELECTRICAL INSTALLATIONS

If you own a new boat, you may be lucky and find that the owner's manual includes an electrical schematic. If not, one of the best things you can do is to make one up yourself. Trace each and every wire throughout the boat, marking it as you go and noting it on the schematic. While you're at it, check the installations for any corrosion or faulty connections. When you're anchored in the boondocks and develop a problem, you'll be very glad you went to the work of making a schematic before you left.

Wiring

Voltage drop is a thief of your boat's electrical power. It can happen in the DC system because the batteries are low, but it can also happen in either the DC or AC system because the wire size is too small to carry the required current or the distance is too great. If there is any doubt, always use a larger gauge wire. Table 4-2 gives recommended wire sizes to keep voltage drop to a minimum of 3 percent.

All wiring connections should be made with crimped fittings and then soldered. Wiring should never be run through the bilge area, and all wires should be supported throughout their length by plastic hangers spaced every 12 to 18 inches.

Receptacles and plugs for the AC and DC systems should be distinctly different. At the very least, they should be clearly marked with the DC ones showing a plus and a minus sign. The best way is for each system to have totally different plugs and matching receptacles so it is physically impossible to plug an appliance into the wrong receptacle. Typical household 110-volt appliances—blender, toaster, hair dryer and such—can plug into "typical" outlets, but not DC equipment.

Bonding

All DC systems should be bonded. Bonding helps protect the boat and her fittings from galvanic and electrolytic corrosion, it provides a low resistance path to ground in case of a lightning strike, and it helps minimize radio interference.

Items to be bonded include all engines (the bonding should be connected to the engine negative terminal), metal enclosures of electrical equipment and electronic gear, fuel tanks and fuel deck fittings, and lead-lined battery boxes. Electrically isolated through-hull fittings do not need to be bonded, as long as they are all of the

LOAD CALCULATIONS FOR DC ELECTRICAL SYSTEM

The following method shall be used for calculating the total electrical load requirements for determining the minimum size of each panelboard, switchboard, and their main conductors. Additionally this information may be used to size the alternator or other charging means, and the battery. (See ABYC E-9.9, and ABYC E-10, "Storage Batteries.")

a. List in Column A the loads that must be available for use on a continuous-duty basis for normal operations.
b. List in Column B the remaining loads which are intermittent and will be calculated based on a diversity factor of 10% or the current draw of the largest item, whichever is larger.

Note: *Calculation should be based on the actual operating amperage for each load and not on the rating of the circuit breaker or fuse protecting that branch circuit.*

A

Navigation Lights	_____
Bilge Blower(s)	_____
Bilge Pump(s)	_____
Wiper(s)	_____
Largest Radio (Transmit mode)	_____
Depth Sounder	_____
Radar	_____
Searchlight	_____
Instrumental(s)	_____
Alarm System (standby mode)	_____
Refrigerator	_____
_____	_____
_____	_____
_____	_____

Total Column A _____

B

Cigarette Lighter	_____
Cabin Lighting	_____
Horn	_____
Additional Electronic Equipment	_____
Trim Tabs	_____
Power Trim	_____
Toilets	_____
Anchor Windlass	_____
Winches	_____
Fresh Water Pump(s)	_____
_____	_____
_____	_____
_____	_____

Total Column B _____

```
10% Column B        ⎫ enter larger of these
Largest Item        ⎬ two for Column B
                    ⎭ under totals

Total Load Required
Total Column A _____
     Column B _____
     Total Load _____
```

Battery Capacity

The battery shall have at least the cold cranking amperage required by the engine manufacturer. Additionally the battery shall have a rated reserve capacity in minutes such that:

— for boats with one battery-charging source the battery shall be capable of supplying the total load of Column A for a minimum of 1½ hours, or

— for boats with multiple simultaneous battery-charging sources, the capacity of all charging sources except the largest charging source shall be subtracted from the total load of Column A. The battery shall be capable of supplying the resulting difference for a minimum of 1½ hours.

Note: In order to calculate the required rated reserve capacity use the following formula:

$$Rated\ Reserve\ Capacity\ (min.) \times \frac{Load\ from\ Column\ A\ (Amps \times 1\frac{1}{2}\ (hr.)\ \times 60\ (min.\ per\ hr.)}{25\ (Amperes)}$$

Courtesy of the American Boat & Yacht Council's 1982 "Standards and Recommended Practices for Small Craft."

Table 4-2

Conductor Sizes for 3-Percent Drop in Voltage

Length of Conductor from Source of Current to Device and Back to Source—Feet

12 Volts—3% Drop Wire Sizes (gauge)—Based on Minimum CM Area

Total Current on Circuit in Amps.	10	15	20	25	30	40	50	60	70	80	90	100	110	120	130	140	150	160	170
5	18	16	14	12	12	10	10	10	8	8	8	6	6	6	6	6	6	6	6
10	14	12	10	10	10	8	6	6	6	6	4	4	4	4	2	2	2	2	2
15	12	10	10	8	8	6	6	6	4	4	2	2	2	2	2	1	1	1	1
20	10	8	8	6	6	6	4	4	2	2	2	2	1	1	1	0	0	0	2/0
25	10	8	6	6	6	4	4	2	2	2	1	1	0	0	0	2/0	2/0	2/0	3/0
30	10	8	6	6	4	4	2	2	1	1	0	0	0	2/0	2/0	3/0	3/0	3/0	3/0
40	8	6	6	4	4	2	2	1	0	0	2/0	2/0	3/0	3/0	3/0	4/0	4/0	3/0	3/0
50	6	6	4	4	2	2	1	0	2/0	2/0	3/0	3/0	4/0	4/0	4/0			4/0	4/0
60	6	4	4	2	2	1	0	2/0	3/0	3/0	4/0	4/0	4/0						
70	6	4	2	2	1	0	2/0	3/0	3/0	4/0	4/0	4/0							
80	6	4	2	2	1	0	3/0	3/0	4/0	4/0									
90	4	2	2	1	0	2/0	3/0	4/0	4/0										
100	4	2	2	1	0	2/0	3/0	4/0											

24 Volts—3% Drop Wire Sizes (Gauge)—Based on Minimum CM Area

5	18	18	18	16	16	14	12	12	12	10	10	10	10	8	8	8	8	8
10	18	16	14	12	12	10	10	10	8	8	6	6	6	6	6	6	6	6
15	16	14	12	12	10	10	8	8	6	6	6	6	4	4	4	4	4	4
20	14	12	10	10	10	8	6	6	4	4	4	4	4	2	2	2	2	2
25	12	12	10	10	8	6	6	6	4	4	4	2	2	2	2	2	2	2
30	12	10	8	8	8	6	4	4	2	2	2	2	2	1	1	1	1	1
40	10	8	6	6	6	6	4	4	2	2	2	1	1	0	0	0	0	1
50	10	8	6	6	6	4	2	2	1	1	1	0	0	2/0	2/0	2/0	2/0	2/0
60	10	6	6	6	4	4	2	2	1	0	0	0	2/0	3/0	3/0	3/0	3/0	3/0
70	8	6	6	4	4	2	2	1	0	0	0	2/0	3/0	3/0	3/0	3/0	3/0	3/0
80	8	6	4	4	4	2	1	1	0	2/0	2/0	3/0	3/0	4/0	4/0	4/0	4/0	4/0
90	8	6	4	4	2	2	1	0	2/0	2/0	2/0	3/0	4/0	4/0	4/0	4/0	4/0	4/0
100	6			4	2	2		0		3/0	3/0	4/0	4/0		4/0	4/0	4/0	

same metal, or if they are individually protected by sacrificial zinc anodes.

Bonding is accomplished by running a strip of copper or bronze (a minimum of ¹/₃₂ inch thick by no less than ¹/₂ inch wide) fore and aft the length of the boat. Although it is generally placed low in the boat, it should be kept out of the bilge. Bonded items are connected to this common conductor by wire no smaller than #8 AWG. Figure 4-12 illustrates a typical bonding system.

Lightning Protection

A common misconception among powerboat owners is that as long as they are surrounded by sailboats with tall masts, they are safe. Wrong! I used to halfway believe this "low profile" theory, until we met a couple cruising in a trawler who had sustained *two* lightning strikes, both times while at anchor with sailboats all around them.

Although experts are not 100 percent in agreement about lightning protection, the general consensus seems to be that the boat should be grounded, generally by grounding the mast. Most powerboats do have masts, even if it's just a short one to support the radar. A metal radio antenna can be considered a lightning protective mast as long as it can be grounded. The "mast" needs to be high enough to surround the boat with a zone of protection (Figure 4-13). If the mast is wood, or any other non-conducting material, a lightning rod (Figure 4-14) should extend at least six inches above it.

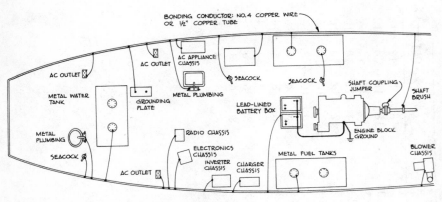

FIGURE 4–12. *Typical bonding system.*

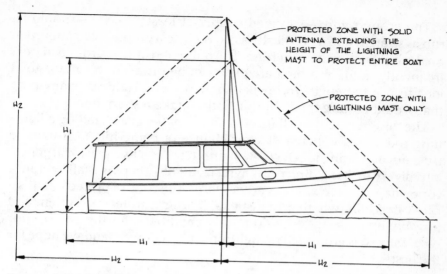

FIGURE 4–13. *If the mast is high enough, it will provide the entire boat with a "zone of protection."*

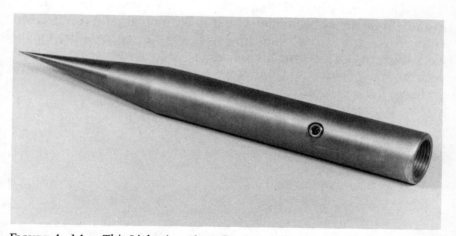

FIGURE 4–14. *This Lightning Chaser™, designed to be mounted on a standard marine antenna mount, will function as a lightning rod and increase the boat's zone of protection. (Courtesy Lightning Electronics, Inc.)*

The ground wire—stranded copper at least 8 AWG—should be run as straight and as vertically as possible to a ground plate mounted on the hull below the waterline. The radio transmitter ground plate is frequently used, or a separate plate can be installed. It's not a good idea to use the engine/propeller shaft, a metal rudder, or anything that would require the lightning path to take a sharp bend.

The disagreement in all this is that many believe installing a lightning rod actually increases your chance of being hit. That may be true, but according to ABYC, "a lightning protective mast will generally divert to itself direct hits which might otherwise fall within a cone-shaped space . . . ," in other words, the zone of protection. It's a tricky decision, whether to install a lightning protection system and possibly invite a strike, or do nothing and hope for the best. In our case, *Duchess* is grounded for lightning protection . . . and we hope for the best.

We all want, and appreciate having, electricity. But a lot of us, myself included, are a little nervous about getting down to the nuts and bolts of adding wiring or tracking down a problem. A healthy respect is good, and certain tasks *should* be left to a professional, but the reality is that once you leave home waters an electrician isn't always handy. Basic wiring really isn't all that difficult, and knowing the rudiments just might mean that someday you'll make a repair and continue on your cruise, instead of tying up for a week or so, waiting for an electrician to put you on his schedule. The more you understand your boat's systems, and the more work you are able to perform yourself, the better off you're going to be.

CHAPTER 5

The Comfort Factor

IF WE'RE NOT COMFORTABLE, cruising won't be any fun. It's as simple as that. Oh sure, there will be times when you're *not* comfortable—when the anchor drags in the middle of a stormy night and you're out on deck in your underwear, with a cold rain beating holes in your skin and you're wondering whose bright idea it was to go cruising in the first place (yours, remember?). But those are the times that make great cruising stories later on, and what is important at the moment is that after the boat is secured you can go below to a cabin that's cozy and warm, a bunk that's snug and dry, maybe jump into a hot shower, or have a cup of hot chocolate. It's called getting comfortable, and many factors enter into the reason why some boats are a joy to cruise on and others are not. Let's take a look.

VENTILATION

I can't say enough about the importance of ventilation, both for the comfort of the crew and the condition of the boat. A good flow of fresh air will mean a boat that's free of mildew, mold, condensation, and stale and musty odors. Many powerboats, with their propensity for large expanses of fixed windows and scarcity of hatches, are sadly lacking in adequate ventilation. Luckily, it's a problem that can be remedied with a small amount of work, and it's work that will repay you tenfold. Figure 5-1 shows a suggested ventilation system for a powerboat.

Ventilators

Cowl vents are the most common type of ventilator on sailboats and older powerboats, and seldom seen on modern powerboats today. I suppose this is because so many boats now have air-conditioning, but cowl vents do their work whether the air-conditioning is running or not—when you're away from the boat and it must be buttoned-up tight, for example. Cowl vents move a tremendous amount of air. The chart in Figure 5-2 shows airflow amounts for both standard cowl vents and the "low profile" type. For best results, they should be installed as pairs—one facing into the wind to direct air below, and one facing away from the wind to remove stale air from the cabin.

To keep water from getting below, cowl vents are usually installed

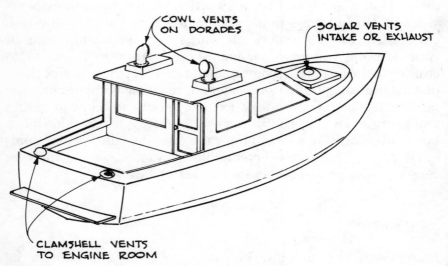

FIGURE 5–1.   *Suggested minimum ventilation system.*

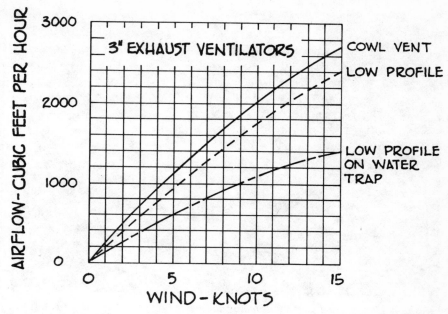

FIGURE 5–2. *Airflow amounts for standard and low-profile cowl ventilators.* (*Courtesy of Nicro Marine*)

on dorade boxes (Figure 5-3). A dorade is simply a box with an internal baffle that allows air to pass, while any water exits through drain holes in the sides of the box. A great idea is to make the top of the dorade out of Plexiglas, so light, as well as air, is brought in. Several manufacturers also make cowl vents with internal baffles that act as a water trap; Nicro Marine offers a water trap vent that incorporates a booster fan (either 12-volt or solar powered) for calm days.

In case you hadn't noticed by now, I am a great fan of solar energy, and one of the best items I've seen is Nicro Marine's solar lo-vent (see Figure 3-4 in the galley chapter), which incorporates a small solar-powered fan for either intake or exhaust. *Duchess* has three of the day-and-night solar vents—one over the shower in the head, one in the galley, and one in the forward hatch. These vents, which fit a 4-inch deck plate, will exhaust over 1100 cubic feet per hour in full sunlight, and continue working at night powered by a ni-cad battery. The solar exhaust vents without a battery will still function at night

FIGURE 5–3.   *A cowl vent mounted on a dorade box, like this one on* Ragtime, *will bring a tremendous amount of fresh air below while keeping water out.*

as long as there is some breeze, since the air passing over the top of the vent will create a vacuum that exhausts air from the cabin.

A hatch is a perfect place for solar vents, since their low profile doesn't create an obstruction, and they keep doing their job even when you're away and the boat is buttoned-up.

Clamshell vents can be placed anywhere that a taller vent would get in the way, but they are most commonly used in conjunction with flexible hose to vent hard-to-reach areas, such as engine compartments, bilges, LP boxes, and interior lockers. They can be mounted on deck or vertically on a cabin side. Like cowl vents, they work best in pairs—one for intake and one for exhaust.

Keep in mind that every part of the boat—not just the living spaces—needs to be ventilated. Hanging lockers, storage lockers, the chain locker, even the bilge—all need air. On a wooden boat, it helps to prevent rot, but it is important on a fiberglass boat as well. When the sun is beating down on a deck, the heat buildup can be enough to ruin cameras, film, or delicate electronics stored in lockers beneath the deck. Obviously you can't run vent hose to every single locker, but you can add metal louvered vents to the doors or cabinet sides, drill ventilation holes, or replace the locker doors with louvered or cane door panels.

If condensation forms inside lockers—a common problem on fiberglass boats—mildew and mold soon follow. This can wreak havoc with your clothes, particularly all-cotton fabrics and leather shoes. A hanging locker should always be well-ventilated. While it can't hurt to add ventilation panels to drawer fronts, I've never had a problem with gear stowed in drawers since there is always airspace around them (Figure 5-4).

On fiberglass boats we've owned in the past, we found it helped a lot to line all the lockers with either carpet or foam-backed vinyl. We would glue the lining to the hull and the underside of the deck, and found it virtually eliminated condensation problems.

Opening Ports

Opening ports and windows provides cross-ventilation. Disadvantages are that they must be closed when it rains, and hull ports must be closed when underway; the cheap ones start to leak in a very short time, and when you open one after a rain you're apt to get a face full of water. Still, I wouldn't be without them.

Ports and windows can often be fitted with a hood so they can be left open in anything but a driving rain (Figure 5-5). These can be of metal, fiberglass, Plexiglas or clear acrylic so they don't block any light. One of my boats had canvas hoods that snapped onto the cabin trunk over the ports. While I had to endure an occasional "Oh, isn't that cute! That boat has eyebrows!," they worked great because they would "give" if they were bumped, so we could always move freely along the side decks.

Several companies, like Bomar and Atkins & Hoyle, to name just two, now make opening ports with a slanted bottom rim that lets water drain away, even if the port is mounted in a sloping cabin side. And often a drain hole can be drilled in the rim to accomplish the same purpose.

Hatches

A hatch will bring in more fresh air than a small port, and ideally a hatch will have two sets of hinges and dogs so it can open either fore

FIGURE 5—4.   *Drawers are excellent for storage since the air space around them prevents condensation and there is little chance for mold or mildew to form. (Photo by Taz Waller)*

FIGURE 5–5. *Windows fitted with a hood, like these Plexiglas ones, can be left open in anything but a driving rain.*

or aft. If a hatch can be opened facing *away* from the wind, it can usually be left open a little bit even in the rain.

Not all hatches must be large enough for a person to fit through. Ventilation hatches are available as small as 10 by 10 inches, usually with clear or smoked acrylic tops to admit light when the hatch is closed (Figure 5-6). Prime candidates for a ventilation hatch are the head and the galley, where both odors and condensation are most likely to cause problems.

In hot weather, most of us open a hatch as wide as it will go. However, if you open it only to about a 45-degree angle, it will create a funnel effect and actually bring more air below.

A wind scoop will bring in vast amounts of air, even when there's just a hint of a breeze. It's more of a challenge to rig one on a powerboat than a sailboat, but it usually can be done. Try running a line from the top of the fly bridge or stack to the bow or stern rail (depending on which cabin you want to ventilate). The biggest disadvantage of a wind scoop happens when a squall passes over at night and you must dash up on deck to take the thing down before it

FIGURE 5–6.   *This model 550S venting hatch from Atkins & Hoyle measures only 6³/₄ inches by 13³/₄ inches inside dimensions, but would do a great job of improving the ventilation in a head or galley. (Courtesy Atkins & Hoyle Limited)*

becomes a rain scoop. But there is no law that says a wind scoop must go inside the hatch. If you installed turn-buttons or snaps on deck around the hatch and sewed their mates to the wind scoop, it could go *outside* the hatch, allowing you to batten down without going topside.

Fans and Blowers

Twelve-volt fans and blowers can provide a good boost to the natural ventilation system, particularly on those sweltering days when there's not a breath of air. A small fan, just to keep the air moving, can mean all the difference between tossing and turning in a sweat-soaked bunk or getting a good night's sleep.

Extractor fans, or blowers, needn't run all the time, but they can be a godsend to remove condensation from the shower compartment, and condensation and cooking odors from the galley. Extractor fans can be added to existing dorade boxes or cowl vents—you can get ones that run off a 12-volt motor or ones that are solar-powered (or both).

A blower is necessary in the engine room, even if you have a water-cooled diesel engine. Long passages, or running a generator for hours on end in hot weather, can raise the ambient temperature in the engine compartment to the point that the efficiency of the engine and other equipment, such as a refrigeration unit, is reduced. And besides keeping the area cool, a blower will extract diesel fumes that might otherwise find their way into living spaces. Be sure that any blower or extractor fan you install is a spark-proof type designed specifically for engine rooms.

AIR-CONDITIONING

Air-conditioning is fast becoming a way of life on modern powerboats. I'm still amazed to find boats as small as 30 feet with a built-in air-conditioning system. Although air conditioners cannot be considered a substitute for adequate natural ventilation, they do offer advantages, one of the biggest being humidity control.

In marinas throughout Florida you'll see boats with household-type air conditioners stuck in hatches. They work fine dockside, but they are not a good choice for a cruising boat. You wouldn't want to make any kind of a passage with an air conditioner in an open hatch, so you have an instant storage problem. And setting it up and taking it down can get to be a real pain.

Air conditioners designed for marine use are the best choice. They are made of noncorrosive materials and are designed to be used with saltwater. There are two types to choose from—self-contained units and modular units. A self-contained unit (Figure 5-7) is precharged and prewired. It is the easiest to install, particularly for the do-it-yourselfer. With a modular air conditioner (Figure 5-8), the compressor is mounted in one place—usually the engine room—and the evaporator and blower located in the cabin. This requires routing tubing through the boat that must be charged with refrigerant after installation is complete—a job best left to a professional. Hooking up

FIGURE 5—7.   *A self-contained air conditioner, like this Sea-King model from Daimen Corporation, is the easiest for a do-it-yourself installation. This model is also equipped for reverse-cycle heating. (Courtesy Daimen Corporation)*

the plumbing is similar for both types, and requires installing additional through-hulls. Figure 5-9 shows a typical installation.

Air conditioners are always rated by BTU's (British Thermal Units). This is the amount of heat required to raise the temperature of one pound of water by one degree Fahrenheit. To figure out how many BTU's you need to cool a cabin, first measure the area to calculate the volume—length × width × height—then multiply by a factor of 15. For example, a cabin measuring 10 feet long by 8 feet wide by 7 feet high would be 560 cubic feet, multiplied by 15 equals 8,400 BTU's. The factor of 15 is recommended by manufacturers, but some dealers consider it to be much too high. You may find that a smaller unit will work just fine, unless you really like living in a refrigerator.

FIGURE 5–8.   *A modular air conditioner allows ducting to be routed to individual outlets in each stateroom or compartment. (Courtesy Daimen Corporation)*

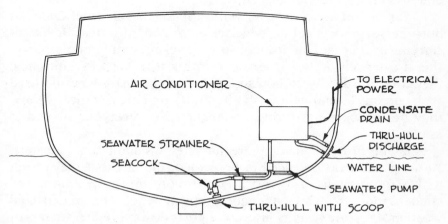

AIR CONDITIONER

TO ELECTRICAL POWER

CONDENSATE DRAIN

THRU-HULL DISCHARGE

SEAWATER STRAINER

SEACOCK

WATER LINE

SEAWATER PUMP

THRU-HULL WITH SCOOP

FIGURE 5–9.   *Typical air-conditioning installation.*

Just keep in mind that the better your natural ventilation is, the less you will need air-conditioning. And you'll find that when you're anchored out, there is almost always more of a cooling breeze blowing on the water than there is ashore.

HEATING

Almost all marine air conditioners are also reverse-cycle heating units. For cruising people heading for warm southern waters, this is undoubtedly all the heat they will need. But if you plan on early spring or fall cruising up north, it may not be.

Reverse-cycle air-conditioning is very similar to a heat-pump system in a house, and their efficiency depends on seawater temperature. The manufacturers of Sea-King air conditioners, for example, state that the heating BTU's are around 20 percent higher than the cooling BTU's, as long as the water temperature is between 55 and 70 degrees Fahrenheit. Below 55 degrees, the efficiency drops. If the water temperature is around 38 degrees or less, you no longer have a heater.

As long as you have 110-volt power available, electric space heaters do a fine job as a temporary heating source. They are small and easily stowed when not in use, yet they will put out as much as 5,000 BTU's. The ones with a blower or fan seem to work better on a boat than the larger, radiant type.

As far as I'm concerned, unvented space heaters, the kind that burn kerosene or alcohol, have no place aboard a boat. It means carrying a fuel that you normally don't use, but more importantly—they are dangerous. If they are not burning at 100 percent efficiency, they produce deadly carbon monoxide, and must always be used with copious amounts of fresh air. Under no circumstances should they be left burning during the night when everyone aboard is asleep.

Catalytic propane heaters are flameless, radiant space heaters. Although they do not need to be vented, the fact that they're not makes me nervous. They do produce moisture in operation, and condensation is always a major problem when cruising in cold weather. Propane heaters also use a great deal more fuel than propane stoves—if they are in constant use, you will be making constant trips to have the tanks refilled.

If you are serious about cold-weather cruising, you should only consider a heating system that is vented. This could be a bulkhead-mounted or free-standing (but bolted down) heater, a forced-air system, or a hot-water heating system. Vented heaters do a good job of removing moisture and pollutants from the air, but they still must be used with adequate ventilation since they are drawing fresh air from the cabin.

Solid fuel heaters, so popular in northern climes, produce a nice, dry heat and can be a good choice as long as the fuel (wood, coal, compressed logs) is easy to get and you have space to stow it. They do tend to be messy, and your cabin top will require frequent cleaning of the soot deposits left by smoke from the chimney.

The cutesy little bulkhead-mounted fireplaces are pretty and fun, but don't expect them to be a real heater. We had one on our last boat and it would take the chill off on a cool evening, and we enjoyed watching the fire and messing around with tending it (it had to be fed about once every hour), but we never expected it to heat the entire boat, or last through the night.

Diesel heaters are a good choice if that is also the main engine's fuel (Figure 5-10). There are a variety of styles to choose from, both bulkhead-mounted and large free-standing ones. They should be mounted as centrally as possible, but in such a way that no one will fall against them or try to grab the hot stack in a seaway. The length of the stack is important for proper combustion, and you must also consider the placement of the smokehead, or Charlie Noble, topside in a place where it will always receive a free flow of air.

The biggest disadvantage of any of these space heaters is that they do not deliver heat evenly throughout the boat. A small electric fan, mounted high next to the heater, will help to distribute the heat in the cabin where the heater is located, but it won't do much for the rest of the boat. For even heat you need either a forced-air heater, or a hot water heating system, and both have much to recommend them.

Forced-air heaters are available that use either diesel or kerosene, with diesel being the obvious choice on most cruising powerboats. Espar and Webasto are two well-known manufacturers of diesel forced-air heaters. The small heating unit can be mounted in a remote location (the engine room or a locker) and the hot air ducted to registers in each cabin, with the temperature controlled by a thermostat. Unlike the space heaters, a forced-air unit can draw air

FIGURE 5—10.   *This vented, drip-feed diesel heater heats a kettle of water as well as the cabin of a 35-foot trawler.*

for combustion from outside the boat, rather than from the cabin, ensuring a constant flow of warm, dry air throughout the interior. Since warm air rises, the registers, or grilles, should be placed as low as possible in each cabin. An added bonus is that any cabinet or locker the ducting passes through will receive some warmth, which will help reduce condensation in those areas.

The forced-air heaters are not only small, but they are fuel efficient as well. For example, Webasto's 11,000 BTU heater, weighing only 14 pounds, uses around .75 pints of diesel an hour at full heat, and consumes less than 3 amps of 12-volt power.

The initial cost of a forced-air unit seems expensive, but over the long haul I believe they are worth the price. And yes, we are installing one in *Duchess* before we head north. Figure 5-11 shows a typical installation of a forced-air heating system.

Hot-water heating systems heat water through a heat exchanger, and pump the hot water to radiators in each cabin. Webasto makes hot water heating systems in addition to forced air. Like the hot air systems, they are thermostatically controlled. They will also heat the domestic hot water supply, and some can be hooked into the engine coolant circuit to provide pre-heating for quick starts in cold weather.

Hot water systems are larger and more complicated than hot air systems, but they are an excellent choice for a large yacht (50 feet and up) requiring a sophisticated system, and with the fuel and electrical capacity to handle the load.

You can figure your BTU requirements just like we did for air conditioning, except you can use a factor anywhere between 10 and 20—10 if you'll always cruise in fairly warm areas, and 20 if you'll be spending a lot of time in the far north. So for most of us, the factor of 15 will be a good average.

COMFORT TOPSIDES

When I'm sitting at home in the dead of winter dreaming about our next cruise, I always picture myself as being outside, enjoying the warmth of the sun and a cooling breeze. Reality is that more often than not it's a hot sun beating down or a hard, driving wind accompanied by rain. Either way, it's not comfortable and most of us are

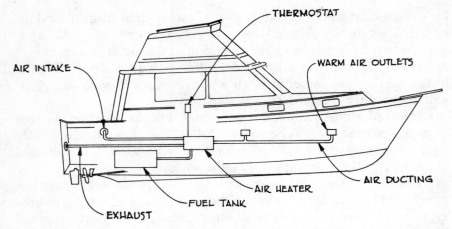

FIGURE 5–11.   *Typical installation of a forced-air heating system.*

soon seeking shelter from the great outdoors. This should not mean, however, that we spend all our time below. The addition of biminis, awnings, and other forms of protection can greatly enhance our cruising comfort.

Protection from the elements will allow us to spend more time topside, and it will also benefit our below-decks comfort. Protecting cabin tops and decks from the sun will keep the interior cooler, by as much as 10 to 15 degrees. An awning that covers ports and hatches will allow them to remain open during a squall.

Biminis

Sooner or later just about everyone with a fly bridge covers it with a bimini. It's a sensible thing to do, considering what we now know about too much sun and skin cancer. Biminis can be fitted with windowed panels for the front, sides and back that will completely enclose it during bad weather (Figure 5-12). The panels should roll up tightly and snap or tie to the bimini edge so they are out of the way when not needed. The aft panel can have a zippered "door" for easy access.

I think you will find these roll-up panels useful in good weather, too. When running at high speeds, the wind in your hair may feel exhilarating at first, but it can get awfully tiring. You may find it's

FIGURE 5–12.   *Joel and Christine Mele's 41-foot Viking,* Christine Marie, *has a beautifully made bimini enclosure. Note the zippered inserts across the front panel that can be rolled up while the rest of the enclosure remains snug. (Photo by Jill Lorenz)*

nice to be able to roll down the front or side curtains to block some of that wind and spray.

Biminis, like all awnings, should have full standing headroom beneath them. I realize that this sometimes gives an unattractive three-story appearance to some boats, especially when all the side flaps are zipped down, but when it's blowing 20 knots and pouring rain, who cares? Comfort first should be the rule.

Awnings

Newer boats often have the after deck covered with a hard top. Furnished with tables and chairs for lounging, these can be wonderful, shady places to enjoy a cooling breeze on a hot afternoon. Fitted with roll-down side curtains, or even just screens, they become a comfortable extra room in all kinds of weather (Figure 5-13). Without the side enclosures, the furniture will soon become ruined from

FIGURE 5–13.   *This covered after-deck has roll-down curtains all around so it can be enjoyed in most any weather.*

rain and sun unless it is either made of plastic, kept covered, or can be folded up and put away (like director's chairs).

If you have a wide-open deck, and are considering a canvas awning, there are several points to keep in mind. It must have standing headroom or you'll find it so uncomfortable that you never use it. You should be able to set it up so it is drum-tight. Otherwise, it will be a constant hassle of running to take it down every time the wind pipes up or a squall threatens. A common arrangement is to install a pipe framework and lace the canvas to the pipe (Figure 5-14). With today's synthetic fabrics, such as Sunbrella and Yachtcrylic, awnings can complement the boat's other canvas work and will last for years.

Small awnings can be made to go over a forward or aft hatch, or to fit along the side decks and cover the ports. Lashed to lifelines or railings, they give protection from sudden rain squalls in hot weather when you want to leave the boat wide open. We use them often when we're anchored out and row ashore for the day. It means we return to a cool, comfortable boat instead of a sauna.

FIGURE 5–14. *An awning laced to a pipe framework will allow it to be stretched drum-tight and prevent flapping on a breezy day.*

Weather Cloths

Weather cloths can also add to your comfort topsides (Figure 5-15). These are simply rectangles of cloth that are lashed between deck and railing around an after deck or bridge deck. They help block wind and spray as well as give a greater feeling of privacy. Weblon, a reinforced vinyl, is most often used since it is waterproof and easy to clean. However, if you don't like its shiny appearance, acrylic canvas will work just as well.

Deck Cushions

Deck cushions should be made of a closed-cell foam, such as Airex, since it does not absorb water and can be left outside all the time. Soggy cushions, or ones that must be stored below when it rains, are a constant pain in the neck on a cruising boat.

Deck cushions are almost always covered with vinyl, but I have come to prefer acrylic canvas covers. Acrylic seems to hold up under hard use as well as vinyl, and is much more comfortable on bare skin.

FIGURE 5—15.   *This 42-foot Grand Banks has canvas work that includes weather cloths around the bridge deck, an aft awning, and a bimini.*

Our vinyl covers, in spite of being "waterproof," trapped moisture inside, creating mildew and its attendent bad odor. Acrylic dries pretty quickly, and since it "breathes" no water gets trapped inside next to the foam.

If you're not ready to replace your vinyl cushions, try using slip-on covers of terry cloth or some other soft, washable fabric. They'll be a lot more comfortable, and the covers can be easily removed for cleaning. The only problem with doing this is that they can be slippery, so don't cover any cushions that are frequently stepped on.

COMFORT BELOW DECKS

While I believe that proper ventilation is the single most important factor in achieving a comfortable interior, there are many other details that make a contribution, from the choice of colors for decorating to whether a bunk cushion is too soft or too hard. Sometimes it's the little things that make the most difference. Consider what most folks do at home when they sit down in their favorite easy chair or sofa. We kick off our shoes and put our feet up, right? If it's your habit too, and you can't do it aboard the boat, you'll soon be making some changes, I guarantee.

Insulation

Insulation can make a big difference in your comfort aboard. It will help the boat stay cooler in the summer and warmer in cold weather. It can greatly reduce, if not eliminate, condensation. It can also make the boat quieter.

I never thought much about noise until we chartered in the Virgin Islands last winter. Taz and I had the forward stateroom, and the bunk was over a large, virtually empty locker. The smallest wave slapping against the hull would reverberate through the cabin like a drum. It took a few nights to get used to it. Granted, if the locker had been chock-full of the usual cruising gear, it wouldn't have been so noisy, but insulation would have helped even more.

Lining the hull inside lockers and cabinets with carpet or foam-backed vinyl will reduce condensation as well as noise. And not just noise from outside, but it acts as non-skid to keep things from sliding around and banging together. This can be done on fiberglass or metal boats, but never on a wooden boat. Wood is a good insulator in itself and lockers seldom need additional lining.

If you're heading for a hot climate, insulating the cabin top and the underside of the deck will keep the interior much cooler. Some manufacturers install a foam-backed vinyl to the overhead that is both attractive and easy to keep clean.

The best insulation material is urethane foam. It comes in rigid sheets that can be cut and glued in place. It must be covered, of course, either with strips of wood for a good-looking ceiling, with painted plywood, or with a vinyl wall-covering.

Decorating

The boat becomes your home while you are cruising, and as such it should be just as cozy and comfortable as the one you left behind (Figure 5-16). Just keep in mind that everything is more compact and therefore subject to more concentrated use than your home ashore. Interior upholstery and carpet will sooner or later get wet, sandy, and stained. We have spilled everything from bottom paint to engine oil aboard our boats, and mostly they have survived it.

There are so many suitable upholstery fabrics available that I couldn't begin to list them all. As a general rule, synthetics or a blend of synthetic and natural fibers are easier to keep clean and hold up to abuse better than all-cotton or all-wool. Look for fabric that's been treated with something to resist staining, such as Scotchgard.

Carpeting, too, should be treated to resist staining, and should be a synthetic or a blend. That includes the backing—natural backing, like jute, will quickly rot aboard a boat. The foam-rubber backing of "kitchen" carpeting doesn't hold up well either. Carpeting does more than just add to a homey feeling. It is an excellent non-skid surface and offers good insulation, particularly in a cabin located above the engine room.

FIGURE 5—16.   *The main saloon on the Hatteras 54 Motor Yacht is as welcoming and comfortable as any living room ashore. Note that the window treatment includes both draperies and venetian blinds. (Courtesy Hatteras Yachts)*

A varnished wooden cabin sole is "traditional," but it does take work to maintain it, and the varnished surface can be slippery. I have seen several yachts with a wooden cabin sole and oriental carpets that were absolutely beautiful. Any such carpet or throw rug, however, must be well secured. If it won't stay in place by itself, secure it with carpet tape, strips of Velcro, or a non-skid underlayment.

Vinyl flooring or linoleum is the best choice for the galley and heads, since it is easy to clean and doesn't mind getting wet. It should be the type that doesn't require waxing. The galley and head are the last places you need a slippery surface.

Curtains or blinds look attractive, but they have practical value as well. They can filter or block the sun on a hot day, and provide privacy, especially when you're dockside. Sheer curtains or venetian blinds will filter the sun and still allow you to view the scenery. Note the window treatment on the boat in Figure 5-16; it has both blinds and curtains.

If you are making curtains, give some thought as to how they will look from the *outside* as well as from the interior. Curtains of a bright color or a bold print look best if they are lined with a plain white fabric that will blend in with the overall topside appearance.

Uninvited Guests

Insects can be the bane of a cruising life-style. To put it bluntly, they can drive you crazy, although *where* you cruise can make a difference. When we lived aboard in Southern California, we almost never needed screens. Then we moved east, and screens became an absolute necessity.

I remember one hot, steamy day on the Chesapeake. When we dropped the hook there was not a breath of air, and black flies—the big ones that bite—descended on us with a vengeance. We jumped below and put in all the screens, but no matter how many we killed there always seemed to be more. That's when we realized they were coming in through the dorade vents. If you need screens, you need them everywhere—hatches, ports, *and* ventilators.

Mosquitoes can be as big a problem as flies in many places. Burning citronella candles or mosquito coils will allow you to sit on deck in the evening, but they should not be burned below decks. If you're going ashore to picnic on the beach, take along a bug repellent spray or you'll be miserable. I know several cruisers who swear that taking daily doses of vitamin B will keep mosquitoes from bothering you. I tried it for almost six months with no luck, but who knows, it just might work for you and anything is worth a try.

In the south, a staple item for sale in most marinas is Avon's Skin So Soft bath oil. I know it sounds strange, but it's a great repellent for no-see-ums—those little guys you can't see but whose bite itches worse than a mosquito's. It is greasy stuff, and we cut it by about half with water, and, of course, when you rub it on you smell just heavenly.

Sea nettles (jellyfish) can be a problem in many places where the water is warm. I won't swim if they're in the water, but a lot of people, including Taz, will jump right in. We keep a supply of meat tenderizer aboard—not for tough cuts of meat, but to apply to jelly-fish stings.

And lastly we come to what can be the worst pest problem of all on a cruising boat—cockroaches. Prevention is the first line of defense. Cleanliness is important, but a cockroach will dine just as happily on paper, glue, or soap as it will on crumbs and table scraps.

Don't bring aboard paper bags or cardboard boxes. They can be hiding cockroach eggs that you'll never see until they've hatched and grown up. Cereal, pasta, and such should not be stored in their original boxes. Empty the contents into glass or plastic containers, or into plastic Baggies, then cut out any instructions and put those into the containers as well. (Adding a bay leaf to dry stores will prevent weevils.) Fresh fruits and vegetables should be rinsed and carefully inspected before they are brought aboard.

Once the boat's been invaded, it's extremely difficult to get rid of every last cockroach, and unless you do, the problem is soon as worse as ever. I know several cruisers who say it's easier to just learn to live with them, but I could never accept this. Even if there is no sign of a roach, we always keep boric acid tablets or "roach motels" spread around in lockers and cabinets—just in case.

Roach bombs can sometimes do the trick, but if you use them the boat must be fogged again in about ten days to kill any newly hatched eggs that were left behind. The problem with this method is that there are so many places aboard a boat for them to hide—much more so than a house—that it is almost impossible to kill every last one. If you have a bad infestation, the only real answer is to call in a professional exterminator.

COMFORTABLE MOTION

Any boat will roll, both at anchor and underway, but rolling is generally more pronounced with a round-bottom displacement hull than with other types. How much you can tolerate, and what, if anything, you choose to do about it is a matter of personal choice.

One solution is to install stabilizers. These are gyro-controlled fins, generally seen on boats 40 feet and larger. They do the job, but at great expense, costing anywhere from $14,000 to $30,000. I would consider them only for a long-range passagemaker. Inshore, maintenance costs can be high because those fins sticking out from the hull are vulnerable to damage. And they are not terribly effective at slow speeds (under 8 or 9 knots).

Another choice might be flopper-stoppers. These are frames, fitted with baffles, that are swung out from amidships on the ends of outriggers or booms. As the boat rolls, the frames, called "fish," offer resistance as the boat tries to pull them out of the water. They can reduce rolling by as much as 40 percent, but they place tremendous strain on the boat and her gear. To add them to an existing boat means that the deck and cabin top, possibly the hull, must be beefed up at the attachment points of mast, outriggers, and rigging. Their big advantage over fins is that they can be used underway or at anchor, although they can be very difficult to retrieve underway if there is any kind of a sea running.

Yet another choice, and one of the best, is a steadying sail. Like flopper-stoppers, the sail can be used both underway and at anchor. John Sheffield, who cruises extensively aboard his Krogen 54 *Dolphin Dancer*, carries both main and mizzen for steadying sails. He reports that the main alone will reduce rolling by about 60 percent, as well as adding ½ knot of speed when reaching or running in 10 knots of wind or better. Especially with a roller furling system (which *Dolphin Dancer* has), sail handling is an easy, one-person task.

*   *   *

The comfort of a cruising boat is composed of many variables. The more thought you give the subject now—before you untie those docklines—the happier you'll be once you're underway and in unfamiliar territory. Like a turtle, your home travels with you and it should be every bit as homey and comfortable as the one you left behind.

CHAPTER 6

The Cruising Tender

ONCE YOU START CRUISING, the ship's tender becomes much more than just another piece of required gear, usually a piece of gear that always seems to be in the way. It becomes a real little workhorse. It's a taxi to get you to and from shore, generally loaded down with people, laundry, groceries, bicycles—you name it, someone will want to take it ashore. Dinghies are great babysitters when you want some quiet time aboard—send the kids to the beach or off for a sail and you'll have the big boat to yourself. When you run aground (we all do, sooner or later), or want to set a second anchor for a coming storm, the tender is pressed into service to row it out. And the tender is often used for exploration—to get you up those little creeks and into coves that are too shallow for the mother ship.

A cruising boat's tender is in constant use, which means it is also subjected to constant abuse. The tender is bumped and bashed by people and gear, dragged up beaches and over rocks, knocked around by other boats at the dinghy dock, left to abrade against rough seawalls, and generally ignored on those rare occasions when it's not being used.

CHOOSING A TENDER

The ship's tender must be chosen with as much care and thought (perhaps more) as any other important piece of gear. Some of the requirements of a good, serviceable tender are:

- It must be of quality construction, sturdy enough to handle the day-in and day-out use demanded by a cruising life-style.
- It must be large enough and stable enough to carry a load in safety and comfort. A load could be everyone in the crew, guests and their luggage, dive gear, groceries, jerry jugs full of fuel or water, bicycles, and the dog.
- It should have enough stability to make getting in and out, or unloading heavy gear, easy and safe.
- It should be capable of traveling long distances, in rough water or against a head wind, and deliver the crew and their gear in reasonably good shape (i.e., dry). It may be calm and peaceful when you go ashore, and blowing blue blazes after a long, friendly night of dinner and dancing. You must be able to get *back* to the boat.
- You should be able to stow the tender aboard, and do it without breaking your back or destroying the mother ship's topsides.
- Ideally, the tender should row well, tow well, have a sailing rig, and perform well with an outboard.

Is there a dinghy that meets every single one of these requirements? Unfortunately, no. It is always a compromise of some sort, and often the "ideal" turns out to be two dinghies, not one. There are two basic choices: a rigid dinghy, or an inflatable, and there are pros and cons to each.

The Rigid Dinghy

I've always preferred a hard dinghy, primarily because I love to row. A quiet sunset "cruise" through the anchorage, or gliding silently along a wooded shoreline listening to birds and looking for wildlife, are pleasures that, in my book, are hard to beat.

The most common rigid dinghy by far is fiberglass, but you will also find them in wood, fiberglass-sheathed plywood, and aluminum. I favor fiberglass because they have a high strength-to-weight ratio, offer low maintenance, and are fairly easy to repair.

Eight feet is the absolute minimum length for a hard dinghy. Anything less is nothing more than a toy and will neither row well nor sail well with more than one person, and it won't have much carrying capacity at all. Bigger is generally better as long as you have room to stow it and it isn't so heavy that smaller crew members can no longer haul it ashore by themselves.

Look for a dinghy with a fine or slightly hollow entry, and a long, straight run to her underbody for both good rowing and towing abilities. A long, very narrow dinghy may be pure joy to row, but if it is the ship's only tender it won't have the necessary stability or load-carrying capacity. The dinghy needs a reasonable beam, and enough freeboard to keep passengers dry in a chop. It should also be equipped with floorboards to keep your shoes, and any gear being transported, dry.

Remember our discussion about displacement vs. planing hulls in the engine chapter? Well, it applies to dinghies, too. Most rigid dinghies are displacement craft so they will never "go fast" or plane like an inflatable will, no matter how big an outboard you put on them. This can be a real disadvantage if you are trying to beat a squall line back to the boat, or want to travel many miles out to a perfect dive spot. Our Trinka dinghy has a small two-and-a-half-horsepower outboard that pushes her at close to hull speed in calm water and less in a chop. There have been times, when trying to row or power against an outgoing tide or a strong headwind, when we wished fervently for a bigger outboard. We're always the last ones there and the last ones back, but I always say we are the best looking. (Taz has since declared that the Trinka is all mine, and he purchased an inflatable for *Duchess*.) There are, of course, rigid tenders, like the larger models of Boston Whalers, that are designed to plane, but these are usually only seen on large yachts.

A rigid tender can generally take a lot more abuse, such as abrasion from seawalls or barnacle-encrusted pilings, than an inflatable. By adding a stainless steel strip to the keel, and runners along the underbody, the dinghy can be hauled up a beach and bounced over rocks—something you would never do with an inflatable. If the bottom becomes foul, it can be scraped and painted with bottom paint, another task that's tricky with an inflatable. There are bottom paints available designed specifically for inflatables—it's scraping barnacles off that requires extra caution.

Hard dinghies display a real disadvantage when you're in a calm anchorage with no wind to keep them trailing astern, or when wind and tide are opposing. They have a bad habit of visiting the mother ship uninvited—a kiss from an inflatable can be a resounding whack from a hard dinghy, risking damage to the ship's topsides as well as the little boat. Sometimes tying it bow and stern alongside, with plenty of fenders, will keep it docile. But I have seen them tied this way in sloppy seas when they bounced around so much they would kick the fenders out of their way, as well as taking on water from small waves formed between the dinghy and the ship. In such a case, about the only solution is to bring them aboard, although there is a device called a Dinghy Whip (Figure 6-1) that is designed to hold off the tender at anchor or underway.

Bringing them aboard can be another disadvantage. They can be more unwieldy, and you run a greater risk of damage to the ship, than bringing aboard an inflatable. Space must be found aboard to

FIGURE 6–1.   *A Dinghy Whip will keep the tender from bumping into the mother ship. It can also be used for towing. (Courtesy Mooring Products Corporation)*

stow them, since they can't be deflated, although in reality hardly anyone ever *deflates* an inflatable.

The Inflatable Dinghy

Inflatables are definitely in the majority as the choice for a cruising boat's tender, and they do have much to recommend them (Figure 6-2). A big advantage is their stability—you can step aboard just about anywhere without capsizing them, and their load-carrying capacity makes them true workhorses. An inflatable's stability and low freeboard makes it easy to board from the water, a real plus for snorkeling or scuba diving.

Another big plus for inflatables is their ability to bob happily (and quietly) all around the mother ship without scraping topsides or putting dents in either boat. This ability is also appreciated by other cruisers when you go visiting around the anchorage.

With the right-size outboard motor, an inflatable will plane, get-

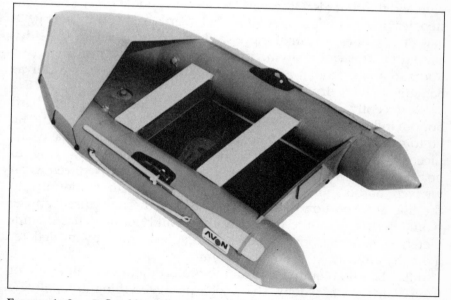

FIGURE 6–2.   *Inflatables are a popular choice for a cruising tender. This 10-foot Rover R3.10 from Avon will take an outboard of up to 10 h.p., and weighs in at only 74 pounds. (Courtesy Imtra Corporation)*

ting you where you want to go in a hurry, in calm seas or rough weather. That can be a real advantage, especially for going long distances, but it can be a disadvantage if the engine quits and you have to row. Rowing an inflatable is like rowing a bathtub—you can do it in good weather, but it can be next to impossible in a stiff wind or choppy seas. Replacing the short, flimsy oars that came with the dinghy with longer, sturdy wooden ones can help a lot, and so can giving the outboard the same attention and care you give the ship's main engine, to make sure it *doesn't* quit just when you need it most.

When you're shopping for an inflatable, don't try to cut corners and save a few bucks—buy for quality. A cheap dinghy may last for years if it is only used on an occasional weekend, but a cruising inflatable will see almost daily service and only a quality one will last the distance. Pay particular attention to the attachment points of oarlocks, towing eyes, carrying handles, and especially the attachment bond on plywood-transom models. These are notorious for pulling loose from the stresses imposed by an outboard engine.

An inflatable must have a firm, reinforced bottom, preferably with plywood floorboards. Otherwise, water will puddle everywhere you step, leaving you with soggy shoes full of grit. And you'll never get a bag of groceries, or anything else, back to the boat in safe, dry condition. This can really be irritating when you've just spent two hours in a laundromat ashore and are heading back with a canvas bag full of clean, dry clothes.

We recently had the opportunity to use one of the new hard bottom inflatables (Figure 6-3), and I must say I was impressed. The bottom was fiberglass, and the inflatable sides Hypalon. It gave us a nice, dry ride, we could pull it up on the beach, and it was as easy to board from the water as any other inflatable. It also towed well when we were harbor-hopping, with the towing eye securely mounted to the fiberglass portion of the dinghy. About the only disadvantage would be that with the hard bottom it could not be deflated completely for stowage, but as I mentioned earlier hardly anyone deflates a dinghy anyway, so it's a moot point.

Inflatables do require extra care to protect them from abrasion, or from damage caused by sharp objects—everything from diving spears to rocks. An inflatable should always be *carried* up a beach, well clear of any surge or incoming tide. It's usually better practice to leave it anchored, take off your shoes and wade ashore. A hard

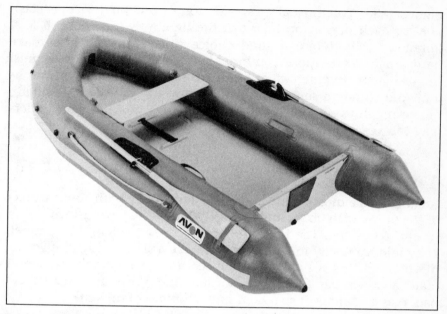

FIGURE 6–3. · *Avon's R.I.B.* (*Rigid Inflatable Boat*) *3.10 combines a fiberglass V-bottom with inflatable hypalon sides.* (*Courtesy Imtra Corporation*)

dinghy left to rub against a seawall may scruff up her topsides, but an inflatable treated this way can wear a hole in the inflated tube in surprisingly short order.

EQUIPPING THE TENDER

A cruising tender needs a lot more gear than just a pair of oars and/or an outboard engine and fuel tank. For starters, it must comply with all Coast Guard safety regulations. These vary with the size of the boat, but remember that when you add the outboard it legally becomes a "powerboat," not simply a dinghy.

Safety Equipment

It is now the law that all boats, regardless of size, must carry approved distress signals. Boats under 16 feet need only carry approved night signals. You must also carry personal flotation devices (PFDs), one for each person on board. If the dinghy is less than 16 feet, flotation cushions are a good choice since they can also make hard dinghy seats more comfortable. Over 16 feet and you must carry an approved life vest or jacket for each person, plus one cushion. And common sense would tell us to carry at least a flashlight, not so much to see where we are going but so other boats underway can see *us*.

Anchoring Gear

An anchor is a must on the cruising tender, along with about six feet of ¹/₄- or ⁵/₁₆-inch chain and at least 50 feet of ³/₈- or ¹/₂-inch three-strand nylon line. The best type of anchor is a collapsible grapnel. They fold up neatly for stowage and have a sliding ring that covers the pointed flukes—an important feature for inflatable owners. I made a canvas bag for our anchor and line. Without it, we always had a tangled mess of spaghetti in the bottom of the dink.

Bailer

Another necessity is a bailer, although a hand pump may be a more efficient choice on a large tender. The most common and perfectly sufficient bailer is a Clorox bottle with the bottom cut out. Attach a line to the handle and tie it to the dinghy or it will never be there when you need it.

Cleats

While inflatables generally have ample attachment points, many hard dinghies have a cleat on the bow and none on the stern. Stern cleats are necessary for tying the dinghy bow and stern alongside the mother ship or a dock, for setting a stern anchor to keep the dinghy off a beach or away from a wharf, and they are invaluable if you are using the tender to set out a second anchor for the big boat or giving the kids and their windsurfer a tow when the wind has died. Don't get cute little plastic or pot metal dinghy cleats, get ones with the heft to do the job.

Repair Kits

Although it doesn't have to be carried aboard the tender itself, you'll want a repair kit for each type of dinghy you have. Kits for inflatables are usually supplied by the manufacturer and include both repair material and adhesive. For fiberglass dinghies, carry cloth, resin, and hardener.

Sailing Rig

It's not a necessity, but a sailing rig for a hard dinghy can be loads of fun. They are great entertainment for the kids, and I know a lot of ex-sailors-turned-powerboaters who wouldn't go cruising without one.

Life will be easier, and your decks less cluttered, if all the sailing gear—rudder, tiller, sail, spars, daggerboard, and leeboard (unless the boat has a centerboard)—can be stowed inside the dinghy. Although my Trinka is a rowing model only, several years ago we had a sailing dinghy with an aluminum mast that was made in three sections. It was a simple matter to put them together, and apart they stowed easily beneath the center seat.

Glass-bottom Bucket

I know this is hardly a necessity, but if you are cruising anywhere that the water is clear enough for snorkeling, a glass-bottom bucket can provide hours of fun. And they do have practical uses. If you're not sure about how well the anchor is set, and don't feel like diving on it, the bucket will quickly show you if it has dug in or not. For locating items dropped overboard, like eyeglasses or keys, a glass-bottom bucket can be a great help.

The wooden buckets, so popular in the Bahamas, are lovely but they can bash around and be a bear to stow. I've seen several people simply cut a large circle out of the bottom of a plastic bucket and glue on a piece of Plexiglas, which still leaves them with a serviceable deck bucket. An inflatable underwater viewer made by Basic Designs (Figure 6-4), called a SeaView, takes up almost no room when it is deflated and stowed.

FIGURE 6—4.   *The inflatable SeaView underwater has a flexible lens that creates a "zoom" effect to provide a close-up view of the bottom. (Courtesy Basic Designs Inc.)*

SHORE EXCURSIONS

Consider this: When you are anchored out, the tender will spend as much time ashore as you do. Most of us take a little time to plan a trip ashore—what to take, what to wear, what not to forget because it will be a hassle to go back to the boat and get it. It's a good idea to take a little time to think about the tender's needs as well.

Security

It's a sad fact that dinghy and outboard engine theft is a real problem in some areas. Inflatables seem to be more of a target than hard dinghies. Although we've never had a problem, we do know several cruisers who have. I never worry much about pulling into a busy, crowded dinghy dock during the day, particularly when it is obvious that other cruisers are leaving lots of loose gear lying around in their boats. I have found that cruising people, on the whole, do look out for each other. But leaving the dinghy on a deserted beach for several hours, or at a lonely dock at night, does concern me sometimes.

The harder you can make it for someone to steal the dinghy in the first place, the less likely they are to try. You can now buy locks for most brands of outboards, and locking the outboard is always a good idea. A length of vinyl-coated chain run through the towing eye and secured with a padlock to a piling or cleat on a dock, or even around a tree, is a good deterrent.

The tender should always have the name painted on as well as the registration numbers. I know it's popular to think up clever names for the tender, and I've seen some great ones, but when you're off cruising it is much better to identify the tender by the name of the mother ship. If someone finds a lost dinghy (they do go off on their own sometimes), it will be much easier for them to return it if they know the name of the big boat. Just put T/T ("tender to") and the name of your boat. Most chandleries carry special paint that can be used on inflatables.

You can go a step further and carve or engrave the name and/or registration numbers—on the transom if it's wood or fiberglass, or on a seat. If you make the lettering very small on the underside of a seat, it is likely to go unnoticed by a thief but it will certainly help to identify the boat as yours if it is ever found.

Shore Landings

Beach landings are easy enough when it's calm, but if there is a surge it can be rough on the tender and sometimes wet for the passengers. I said earlier to anchor the dinghy, take off your shoes and wade ashore—but I would like to add a note of caution here. If the beach is just sand, and you can see the bottom, bare feet are probably all right. But if you can't see the bottom, or it's rocky or you know the water is polluted, wear shoes. Everyone who goes cruising should have at least one pair of old, beat-up sneakers for wading and beachcombing. Several years ago, a good friend of mine was cruising in the Chesapeake. He cut his foot while pulling the tender ashore. It seemed minor at the time, but the resulting infection put him in the hospital for over a month. It sure made believers out of this crew.

A hard dinghy can be dragged up a beach, but it is better to carry it. And an inflatable should always be carried. Take it above the tide line, and then secure the painter to a tree, a rock, or whatever is handy. If nothing is available, you can set the anchor on the beach and dig it in with your foot.

An inflatable, designed to be *in* the water, where it is supported fully and evenly, is always better off left at anchor. Take it ashore and you run the risk of poking the bottom with a rock, a piece of glass or coral, or other debris. And never load gear into an inflatable while it is on the beach—get it floating and then load it.

Anchoring a dinghy does not necessarily mean you must wade ashore. When you get close to land, drop the anchor from the stern. Then drift straight in to the beach, jump out, and tie the painter from the bow to a point that will keep the dinghy at an angle to the shore (Figure 6-5). This also works for tying off a seawall.

If you must tie up the tender at a dock with jagged edges, or a very crowded one, (or when the weather is rough enough to slam the dinghy against the pilings), setting a stern anchor can help keep the boat out of harm's way. If you tie up alongside using bow and stern lines, you can sometimes set the anchor as a breast hook to hold the dinghy off the dock.

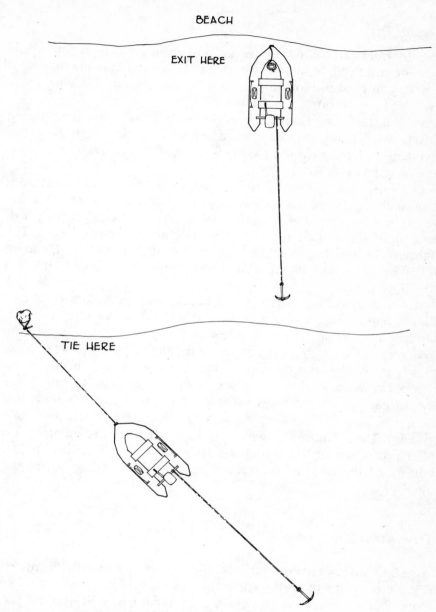

BEACH

EXIT HERE

TIE HERE

FIGURE 6–5.   *Anchor a dinghy off the beach by first dropping the anchor from the stern. Then drift in to the beach and tie the painter from the bow to a point that will keep the dinghy at an angle to the shore.*

Keeping Dry

Dinghy rides can sometimes be wet and woolly affairs. If you're in a bathing suit heading out to a dive spot, it doesn't really matter. But if you're going ashore for dinner, or returning to the boat with groceries and dry laundry, it does matter.

With a hard dinghy running under outboard power, just slowing down will usually stop or greatly reduce any spray. On the other hand, an inflatable running at planing speeds is generally dryer than at slower speeds.

Obviously if it's raining you'll go ashore in foul weather gear, but rain or shine it's always a good idea to take along at least a jacket if you'll be ashore for a long stretch. Weather can change awfully fast, and more often than not we've been glad we remembered. The lightweight windbreakers, like the ones sold by Lands' End, can be rolled up into a tight little package and stuffed anywhere, even left in the dinghy.

Another item I try to remember to take is a small, dry towel in a Ziploc plastic bag. It can be used to dry your feet after a beach landing, or to wipe the evening dew off the seats after a night ashore. When you're on a shopping expedition, take along a couple of large plastic trash bags to protect your purchases on the ride back.

Most of us are avid picture-takers when we're cruising, and keeping the camera dry is always a worry. Waterproof pouches are worth their weight in gold for keeping cameras, or any other valuables, safe and dry. The inflatable pouches will float when they're inflated, and offer protection to the contents if they are knocked around in the bottom of the boat or dropped when you are getting out of the dinghy.

TOWING THE TENDER

For short hops between harbors, the tender can usually be towed (Figure 6-6). It's often the easiest path to take, but you do have to remember it's there when you stop to anchor or pull into a dock. Then the tender needs tending, and fast, before the painter gets sucked into the props.

Polypropylene line can be used for the towline since it floats, but I

FIGURE 6–6.   *The tender can usually be towed when harbor-hopping, particularly if the weather is good. Note here that the towing eye is securely mounted to the fiberglass portion of this rigid-bottom inflatable.*

don't like it because it deteriorates rapidly in sunlight or from chafe, and it is noted for untying itself. Nylon line is really the best, and spacing cork floats along its length will keep it from sinking. A towline that floats will work when you are underway or reducing speed slowly, but it may not be enough when you are backing down to set a hook. The tender should always be brought up close when anchoring or maneuvering, to make very sure you don't foul the props. Sometimes it's better to tie it alongside.

Taz and I have logged thousands of cruising miles, almost all of them with the tender in tow. And we've gotten into enough trouble to no longer feel comfortable doing so except for very short distances. The problem is there is no guarantee that the weather will hold for the length of the passage. After one summer's cruise in the Chesapeake, we left St. Michaels, Maryland, heading for home in North Carolina. We had planned on a short day's run and anchoring for the night, but it was a beautiful evening and NOAA (the National Oceanic and Atmospheric Administration, which provides continuous, twenty-four-hour weather broadcasts on VHF radios) gave a good weather forecast, so we decided to continue through the night. By 0200 the wind was howling 30 knots right over the transom. Our towed dinghy came surfing down the waves and slammed into us with a vengeance, over and over (hard enough to crack the fiberglass bow, we later discovered). We could not find a towing position—close up, far away, or alongside—that would stop the assault. In those conditions we were not about to try to hoist her aboard. By the time we reached Norfolk, the dinghy was not only bashed but full of water and acting like a large sea anchor.

Aside from "never trust NOAA," there are several lessons to be learned here. We should have brought the dinghy aboard as soon as we made the decision to keep going—in daylight and while the weather was calm. And every tender that is towed should have a drain or some type of self-bailer. A swamped dinghy can be more than a sea anchor; it can be a real danger. If it were swept beneath the mother ship, it could easily wreck the prop or rudder, and then you would be in serious trouble.

If you do elect to tow the tender for a long distance, it should have two painters, one attached to the towing eye and one attached to a bow cleat, with each line led to a separate stern cleat on the big boat. The lines will function as a bridle to help the tender stay in position, and if one parts you'll have a backup. Keep in mind that towing a dinghy behind a high-speed powerboat will place tremendous strain on the dinghy's fittings, and you may need to add reinforcement to the attachment points.

BRINGING THE TENDER ABOARD

There are so many aids available today that bringing the tender aboard should never be a backbreaking proposition. The easier and faster you can do it, the more likely you'll be *to* do it, even for a short passage.

Stern davits have long been popular, and for good reason (Figure 6-7). They make lifting the tender quick and easy, since it isn't coming all the way aboard. Adding a winch will make the chore easier yet, even for the kids. About the only disadvantage is that it is impossible to use a swim step unless the dinghy has been lowered. The dinghy should never be longer than the transom is wide, or someday you'll wrap it around a piling when leaving a fuel dock.

Several companies, among them Edson Corporation and Venture Marine, make lifting devices that can be mounted on a swim step to allow an inflatable to be pulled up on the step and held vertically against the transom (Figure 6-8). They appear to be quite simple to use, although, unlike davits, the outboard would have to be removed before the dinghy was hoisted. Some of them can also be used for a hard dinghy.

A tender stowed on deck, or on a cabin top, will require a cradle or some kind of chocks to hold it securely in position (Figure 6-9). If the boat has a mast and boom for a steadying sail, the rig can be used as a cargo boom to hoist the tender aboard. Otherwise davits will be required, and they must be able to reach far enough outboard to hook up the bridle. Large boats, with big, heavy tenders, will have power-operated davits, or even a hydraulic crane.

FIGURE 6–7. *Stern davits make lifting the tender aboard a quick and easy task.* (*Courtesy The Edson Corporation*)

FIGURE 6–8.   *A lifting device, like this Port-A-Lift from Venture Marine, makes it easy to stow an inflatable securely against the transom. (Courtesy Venture Marine Inc.)*

I like stowing the tender upright, since it eliminates the not-always-easy step of a 180-degree roll. However, it does mean that the dinghy must be fitted with a cover and ridgepoles to keep water from puddling in the center of the cover. An upright tender is a great place to stash all kinds of gear—dinghy equipment, sailing rig, fenders, dock lines, all sorts of stuff. An upright tender should also have a drain, particularly if it is on stern davits and not supported by chocks.

Choosing the right tender for a cruising boat is not a simple decision, and my vote is always for two—a hard dinghy for rowing and sailing, and a good inflatable for the heavy-duty work. While two tenders are a must if you cruise with children, they are awfully nice just for a

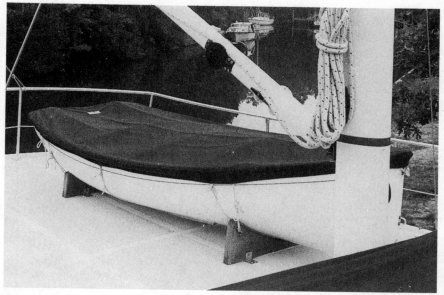

FIGURE 6–9.   Joan M's *tender is a 10-foot Trinka, stowed securely in chocks on the bridge deck. The well-fitting cover goes over ridgepoles to keep water from puddling in the canvas.*

cruising couple. It gives you the freedom to go ashore without leaving your partner feeling stranded. And you will have one in service while the other one is being repaired or repainted. A good tender is so important to a cruise that it is worth the time and effort (and money) spent getting a good one—and giving it the care it deserves.

CHAPTER 7

Taking Your Toys

CRUISING IS MORE than just viewing the scenery, beautiful though it may be. Time is spent ashore, exploring new sights and shopping in new towns. Time is spent working on the boat, performing routine maintenance and small repair jobs. But a great deal of time is spent doing what a lot of us workaholics refer to as "nothing": swimming, snorkeling, reading, napping, needlework, or watching old movies on the VCR. Indeed, just *having* the time to pursue these leisure activities is a big reason why a lot of us go cruising.

Almost all activities require a certain amount of equipment, some more than others (if napping is high on your list, everything you need is already aboard), but small bits of gear here and there can add up to a pile of stuff. It all must be stored somewhere so it is secure underway and easily accessible when you want it.

TOYS ON THE WATER

In the last chapter we talked about the value of having two dinghies, one for a workhorse and one for the pleasure of rowing or sailing.

I've seen large motor yachts carrying three and four or more, just to keep everyone aboard happy.

Sailboards

Sailboards are extremely popular today, and you'll see them aboard cruising boats of every size, and on powerboats as often as sailboats. They can be both great fun and a great source of exercise. The only drawback is their unwieldy size, which can make them tough to stow where you won't be running into or tripping over them.

Lashing them forward along the lifelines can work as long as they don't interfere with handling docklines or anchoring chores. Several companies, such as Nautical Engineering and Johnson Marine, make racks for sailboards that are designed to mount against the lifeline stanchions (Figure 7-1). When Taz and I were living in California aboard *13 Keys*, a 40-foot motorsailer, his son kept his sailboard lashed to the lifelines. It was a secure and out-of-the-way place, except that it completely blocked the view from two of the ports.

They can sometimes be laid flat on a cabin top, provided you have a cabin that is long enough. Another good method might be to tie the sailboard along the rails of a bridge deck. They are lightweight enough that it shouldn't be a problem getting one up there. If you have the muscles to windsurf, you have the muscles to hoist it aboard and put it away.

Rowing Shells

We know several people who are avid rowers. For them, rowing a dinghy is just not enough, and they carry rowing shells aboard. These can be even harder to stow than a windsurfer. The smallest ones are around 16 feet long—although, like the windsurfer, they are lightweight. The Alden single, for instance, at 16 feet weighs only 40 pounds. Complete with the Oarmaster rowing unit, the cost is around $1,750.

Besides stowing the shell itself, space must be found for the bulky sliding seat and rigger assembly. A fiberglass shell is probably the better choice, since it will require less maintenance and take more abuse than the lovely but fragile wooden shells.

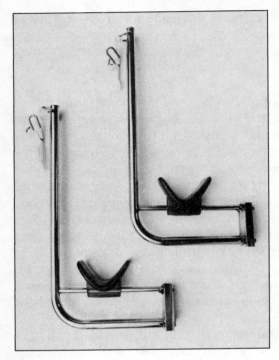

FIGURE 7—1.   *These stainless-steel sailboard carriers, at $178.50 a pair, make it easy to mount a sailboard securely against the lifelines. (Courtesy Nautical Engineering)*

Alden also makes a 16-foot double-ended rowing boat, the Appledore, which disassembles into two sections that nest together to occupy less than nine feet of deck space. Like the shells, it can be rowed with the sliding seat assembly, and there is a sailing rig available for it as well.

Personal Watercraft

Another small boat that is becoming all too common is the water scooter, or jet bike, or personal watercraft—whatever you choose to call them. I choose to call them a menace. The noise they make is deafening, the wake they leave is horrendous. I'm not the only one who feels this way. An increasing number of states and towns are passing tight restrictions limiting the use of personal watercraft. Oliver Moore, publishing director of *Yachting* magazine, refers to them as "the aquatic equivalent of no-see-ums."

If you want to be shunned by everyone in a peaceful anchorage, launch one from your boat and take it for a ride. It's not just the boats that are so offensive, but the seeming rudeness of those who use them. If you are thinking of taking one along to entertain teenagers aboard, take a windsurfer or a sailing dinghy instead. In the long run, everyone will be happier.

Water Skis

While on the subject of rudeness, I would like to also mention waterskiing. It can be fun, if you have a tender large enough to tow skiers. But a crowded anchorage, with dinghies coming and going and people swimming from their boats, is no place for a fast, noisy ski boat leaving a big wake. If you are going to ski, go out into open water and away from busy harbors and anchored boats.

TOYS IN THE WATER

Once we get to warm weather and warm water, Taz and I spend almost as much time in the water as we do aboard the boat. After our last cruise, which included three months in the Bahamas, I concluded that we were part fish. Luckily, with the exception of scuba diving, most water activities require little in the way of equipment—just jump in and enjoy.

Swimming

Swimming, one of the best of all exercises, requires only the ability to swim, a bathing suit (sometimes not even that), and a way to easily get in and out of the water.

There are as many varieties of swim ladders as there are boats. If your boat has a swim platform off the transom, you will still need a ladder to get out of the water. These can be the kind that are permanently mounted and fold up when not in use, or one that can be removed and stowed elsewhere.

Without a platform, the most common arrangement is a ladder hung from the railing either amidships or aft over a flat transom. Some are designed to slide into brackets mounted on the hull; others are simply hooked over the rail. If you have a wooden toe rail and choose the latter, be sure it is made so it won't mar the finish of the wood.

Ladders today are usually anodized aluminum or stainless steel, although you can still find ones of teak or mahogany for traditional powerboats. The inexpensive plastic ladders are generally not sturdy enough for day-in day-out use on a cruising boat. So-Pac makes two styles of ladders—both clip-on and over-the-rail—of hefty 316 stainless steel, although their range of sizes is limited. American Ladder Corporation, on the other hand, offers an extensive choice of styles and sizes of folding ladders constructed of stainless steel and anodized aluminum.

Be sure the ladder has wide, flat steps, not just round metal rungs. Your bare feet will thank you every time you step on one. The ladder should be long enough to have at least two steps completely submerged; three are even better. If the hull has a lot of flare, the ladder will need stand-offs of some type to hold it away from the boat—otherwise it will be very difficult to get aboard, and hard on fingers and toes as well.

If you have trouble getting into an inflatable from the water (I sometimes do if I'm not wearing swim fins), at least one company—American Ladder Corporation—makes a folding ladder designed specifically for inflatables. I haven't tried one yet, but it sure seems like a fine idea.

Inflatable rafts, the kind sold in drugstores and department stores in resort areas, are fun for just drifting around, or to take a rest in the water after swimming twenty laps around the boat. And they will keep kids entertained for hours. Deflated, they roll into a tight bundle and take up almost no space in the locker.

Diving

If you're cruising where the water is warm and clear, snorkeling will open up a whole new world of breathtaking beauty. Spectacular coral formations, sea fans, brightly colored fish darting through the sea grass—it's all there for the viewing, and it requires only a mask, snorkel, and fins. You don't even have to dive. I can spend hours just drifting slowly along on the surface, taking it all in.

Don't bother with the dime-store-variety mask and fins. Go to a dive shop where a qualified clerk (they are almost always divers themselves) can help you select a mask that's a perfect fit. A mask that leaks is useless. They can also recommend fins for the type of diving you plan to do. You'll pay more at a dive shop—$50 and up— but the quality and fit are worth the price.

Most people who wear glasses find that the mask gives enough magnification to enable them to see fine underwater. However, if your eyesight is really bad (like mine), you can have prescription lenses made by an optician that fit inside the dive mask. Mine snap into a small plastic bracket glued to the top of the glass on the inside of the mask.

We keep our gear stowed in mesh dive bags (Figure 7-2). The bags keep everything together for storage, are easy to grab when it's time to go diving, and are handy for shell-collecting and beachcombing expeditions.

Scuba diving will open the underwater world even further, although it requires greater skill and a lot more equipment. You must attend classes and pass a test to become certified, and you cannot get

FIGURE 7–2.   *Mesh dive bags are great for diving and beachcombing expeditions. I always include an old pair of shoes as standard equipment—for walking in the surf, around coral, and on rocky beaches.*

a tank filled unless you *are* certified. Classes typically include twelve hours of class instruction and twelve hours of pool instruction followed by several open-water dives, and cost around $150 to $200.

Once you have taken the course and purchased all the gear—wetsuits, tanks, regulators, BCs (buoyancy compensators), etc.—you will have made a sizable investment, close to $1,000 or more. And of course you also have to find storage space for all of it. However, you can view the investment as insurance as well as fun. The ability to dive will allow you to make underwater emergency repairs to prop, shaft, or through-hulls, and it's a great way to keep the bottom clean between haulouts.

There are a few other items that are essential when diving, whether scuba or snorkeling. The sun's rays are intensified in the water and you can get a severe burn before you know it, particularly when you are swimming leisurely along the surface looking at the bottom. If I'm spending much time in the water, I always wear a lightweight T-shirt to protect my back and shoulders. Sunscreen lotion is also important, until you get very tan. My preference is a product called Bullfrog. You won't always find Bullfrog in a drugstore, but you will find it in dive shops, and sometimes in marine hardware stores. It is slightly greasy, but it does not come off in the water and seems to offer more protection than any I have tried. The last item is a pair of dive gloves. Some corals and shells are poisonous, or can deliver a bad sting. Don't pick up or touch *anything* unless you are wearing gloves, and never pick up a shell unless you can identify it as being non-poisonous. Garden or work gloves are all right, but dive gloves, while more expensive ($15 to $25), will provide a better fit and last longer in the marine environment.

TOYS ASHORE

When we go cruising, most of us rediscover the lost art of walking. A leisurely stroll gives us the time to stop and smell the roses, to chat with local people and learn more about them and their way of life. But sometimes it is nice to have another means of transportation, a "shore toy" if you will. It can greatly increase your traveling range ashore, and make shopping expeditions faster and easier. Marinas and anchorages aren't always located near shops or the post office, and while many marinas do have courtesy cars, it's not something you can count on. And sometimes it's just fun to go exploring farther inland, past the mile or two you can comfortably walk.

Bicycles

Everyone I know with bicycles considered them toys when they bought them and a necessity after they had cruised with them. The choice is between a standard bike and a folding bike. Joan and Clarence Hyde carry a pair of standard bicycles aboard their Krogen 42, *Joan M*. The bikes are kept on the bridge deck and after several years of cruising they are quite rusty (Figure 7-3), but as Joan points out, they bought them used three years ago for $15 each and they are still going strong, so why worry about a little rust?

Folding bikes are just that. They fold up into a tidy package that is more easily stowed, or lifted on and off the boat, than a full-size bicycle. Serious bikers may insist on taking along the fancy ten-speed racer they rode at home, but most of us find that a simple, three-

FIGURE 7–3. *Joan and Clarence Hyde carry their bicycles on the bridge deck of their Krogen 42. The wire baskets will hold a lot of gear, and fold flat against the rear of the bike when not in use.*

speed bike that will fit in the dinghy, or in a locker, and that can stand to be knocked around a little bit, will do just fine.

Most folding bikes will collapse to around 34 by 30 inches and a thickness from 10 to 17 inches. They can weigh anywhere from 22 pounds to 35 pounds. If a carrying case with handles does not come with the bike, it's a good idea to make one. Besides being easier to carry, it will be easier to stow without all those parts sticking out to catch on things. Any bike stowed on deck should have a canvas cover to protect it from the elements.

Rather than just ordering bicycles through a mail-order catalogue, it's better to try out a few at a bike shop first. Some of them are a lot easier to collapse and assemble than others, and the only way to find out what you consider easy or difficult is to try it yourself. A number of the folding bikes have small wheels—16 or 17 inches, which makes them harder to steer and rougher riding than a bike with standard-size wheels. Not everyone objects to this, but I prefer larger wheels—20 to 26 inches. Balloon tires are the best on rough dirt roads, or on gravel or coral paths.

You'll find folding bikes made of aluminum, painted or chromed steel, even stainless steel. The aluminum ones are lighter weight and less prone to corrosion, but they all have at least some parts that will rust eventually. One of the most popular is the Round-A-Bout by Peugeot. This high-quality bike, at around $350, has a hi-carbon steel frame, 3-speed gears, 20-inch wheels, and folds to a 30 by 32 inch package.

Another bike, the DaHon, folds to a quite small unit of only 9 by 18 by 28 inches. Different models with a range of gears from one to five are also available. The standard bikes are painted steel and there is a "deluxe" version with a stainless-steel frame. Prices range from $180 to $350. These are good bikes and my only objection to them is the small wheel size of 16 inches.

Since bicycles are frequently used for transporting gear and groceries, be sure they can be fitted with sturdy carriers and/or wire baskets (Figure 7-3). The collapsible baskets are especially nice since they hold a lot of gear when opened and fold flush against the rear of the bike when not in use. Dudley Boycott simply lashes canvas ice bags to the rear carrier to transport groceries or laundry (Figure 7-4).

Bicycles that live in the marine environment do require some care. They should be hosed off with fresh water whenever possible, and

FIGURE 7–4. *Dudley Boycott, from the trawler* Myth, *lashes canvas ice bags to the rear carrier of his bike for transporting gear.*

thoroughly dried before they are stowed. One bike shop recommended coating the entire bike with a spray wax before putting it away. Clean the bike periodically with WD-40 or CRC, then oil the chain and grease the cables with a waterproof grease. With proper care, a bicycle should give you quite a few years of service, even on a boat.

Motorized Transportation

Adding a motor to a bicycle will increase your range even more, although you can no longer consider it "great exercise." These little gasoline motors generally weigh less than ten pounds and can get as much as 200 miles per gallon. Depending on the motor, they will go from 25 up to 35 miles per hour. They are started by pedaling up to a specified rpm, usually 5 to 10 mph (there's your exercise) and then the motor engages. In most places, a motorized bike does not have to be licensed as long as it's under a specified horsepower.

Mopeds and motorcycles are another option, but their weight and size generally make them suitable only on large yachts with the equipment to swing them over the side and ashore. One exception is the Di Blasi moped. Although it weighs a hefty 72 pounds, it can be folded, and it stows neatly in its own carrying case.

TOYS ABOARD

No matter what anyone tells you, including me, you are *not* going to spend all your cruising time ashore or in the water. Many hours will be whiled away below decks, relaxing in your home away from home and just enjoying "being there."

TV and Stereo

Is there a cruising boat out there that does not have a television set? Maybe, but if so, it is an endangered species. Quite a few marinas offer cable hookup at every dock, and many new boats appear to have cabinets that were designed specifically for a television set. Where to put the TV is usually a high priority on the get-ready-to-go list. If it won't fit snugly inside a cabinet, be sure there are chocks around it (Figure 7-5) or some way to secure it when the boat's underway. The last thing you need is an expensive television set crashing onto the cabin sole.

It may be easiest to just take a small TV from the house and put it on the boat, but that will mean using 110 electricity. If you don't want to listen to a generator and the TV at the same time, an inverter will do the job nicely (see the chapter on electricity). The other option is a 12-volt TV. A 12-volt color TV will draw about the same as a light bulb, so there is little drain on the batteries. *Duchess* has a color television that will run off either 12-volt or 110-volt, just by changing the cord. It was more expensive than a 110 model only, but it means we can use it without a generator or an inverter when at anchor, or plug into 110 when dockside.

FIGURE 7–5. *The* Joan M*'s TV cabinet, custom-made by local woodworker Gary Gresko, has chocks to hold the TV securely when underway. The lower shelves are designed to hold a VCR and tapes.*

A television on a boat generally requires an outside antenna. Rabbit ears may work near a big city, but out in the boondocks reception is apt to be poor. There are several companies, such as Shakespeare and Dantronics, that make fully enclosed, weatherproof antennas for marine use (Figure 7-6). Your best choice is an omnidirectional model so you don't have to fiddle with a rotor or make frequent trips topside to adjust the antenna.

Most of the antennas are designed to be mounted on either a horizontal or vertical surface. The higher you can place them the better they will work, and they should be mounted as far as possible from other antennas to avoid distortion or interference. They will provide reception up to 50 miles, sometimes farther.

VCRs are almost as popular aboard boats as television sets. I predict that the day will soon come when cruising people trade old movies the way we now trade paperback books. Aside from the cost of tapes, there is no reason not to take along a stash of your favorite flicks, or video games and children's programs if you are cruising with kids.

There is still a part of me that can imagine cruising without television, but not without a stereo (Figure 7-7). Although you can buy, at

FIGURE 7–6.   *Shakespeare's 2010 marine TV antenna is omnidirectional and operates on either 12 or 24 volts DC. (Courtesy Shakespeare Company)*

a hefty price, a record player that will work aboard a boat, storing records could be a real headache. It is easier, and takes up a lot less room, to put everything on cassette tapes. There are also any number of companies that make weatherproof speakers, so you can enjoy music out on deck or on the flying bridge.

Cassette tapes, and videotapes, too, must be stored with care. They will deteriorate rapidly from excessive heat or moisture, so they must be kept in a cool, dry area. This means never in a locker right under the deck, or on a shelf where the sun beats in for most of the day. If condensation is a concern, store them with small packets of silica gel or some other type of moisture absorber.

Books and Hobbies

Not all books belong in the toy category. We carry dozens of books as a permanent library—cruising guides, navigation books, how-to repair books, cookbooks, and quite a few reference books on shells,

FIGURE 7–7. *For many cruisers, going without a good stereo system, like this one aboard the* Christine Marie, *is just about unthinkable.* (*Photo by Jill Lorenz*)

fish, plants, birds, and other wildlife. It's those other books, the ones my friend Lizzie refers to as "penny awfuls," that are not exactly necessary but have a place on a cruising boat, anyway.

Taz and I both seem to always be too busy ashore to do much reading, but we make up for it when we cruise, and we'll go through several hundred books on a long cruise. And no, I don't go out and buy that many paperbacks before we leave. We start out with a good selection, and count on trading as we go. Most marinas that cater to transients have a paperback exchange—leave a book and you can take one. You'll always find a lot of trash on the shelf, but after a while I'll read anything. And rowing around an anchorage with a stack of books to trade is a great way to meet new people.

It's also a good idea to take along a deck of cards and a few games like checkers or chess, Monopoly or backgammon. You may never play cards or games at home, but on a rainy afternoon at anchor they may be just the ticket, especially if you have guests aboard who expected to spend the week sunbathing.

Hobbies that you enjoyed at home will be enjoyed just as much when you cruise—within reason, of course. My hobby of gardening does not exactly lend itself to shipboard life, except for a couple of houseplants. But I always stash away a few needlepoint projects, and Taz brings his carving tools and small pieces of wood. Even if we never get them out, it's nice to know the option is there.

Cameras

A camera is just about a necessity on a cruising boat. If you cruise without taking snapshots, I guarantee you will regret it. Years later, a scrapbook full of memories can bring back the happy feelings of the cruise like nothing else—there is just no substitute for pictures of places visited and new friends met along the way. If you're a diver, a waterproof camera (Figure 7-8) will add to the fun. A waterproof camera is also handy for shooting in rain or spray. Several of the well-known camera companies, such as Minolta and Canon, make underwater cameras. Prices range from around $150 for 110 cameras to $300 and $400 for 35mm models.

The camera lens should always be protected by a filter. When you are shooting aboard, you'll be constantly wiping spray off the lens, which can scratch it and will eventually wear off the coating. It's better to abuse the filter, which can be easily replaced. An ultraviolet filter can be used for outdoor shots; and on bright, sunny days on the water a polarized filter will reduce the glare from reflected light and give you truer color.

There is one cardinal rule of marine photography: Keep your horizon level. I can't tell you how many otherwise great shots I have ruined by forgetting this one simple rule. It is all too easy to focus on the subject and forget that you are on a moving (never level) boat. When Taz and I were at the Long Island Regatta in the Bahamas, we followed the racers in a friend's inflatable. Everyone got beautiful pictures, except me. In mine, the boats appeared to be straight up, and the horizon on a heel!

Like cassette tapes, camera and film must be stored in a cool, dry place. Film is particularly sensitive to heat and moisture. Try to get it developed as quickly as possible. We carry Mystic Color Lab mailers aboard and send the exposed film off at every opportunity. Although

FIGURE 7–8. *A waterproof camera is great for shooting in rain or spray as well as for diving. This Minolta Weathermatic Dual 35 is completely automatic and good down to 16 feet underwater—and it also floats. (Courtesy Minolta Corporation)*

I've never tried it, some photographers recommend keeping exposed film in the refrigerator if you can't get it developed in a reasonable amount of time.

Just because we refer to something as a "toy" doesn't mean that it is unnecessary. After all, there are some uninformed folks around who would call the boat itself a toy, and we know better than that. Whether it's a bicycle, a camera, or another dinghy—it may be something we could live without, but if it adds to our enjoyment and makes the cruise more fun, and there is room to stow it—why not have it? I am a firm believer in toys—besides being fun, they help us keep our sanity in a crazy world.

CHAPTER 8

Anchoring and Docking

As CRUISING BECOMES more popular, favorite anchorages become more crowded. What is interesting is that these anchorages are no longer the exclusive domain of sailboats. Powerboats are there, too, in ever-increasing numbers. While this is due at least partly to powerboat cruisers' discovering the pleasures of being on the hook, and equipping their boats for freedom from shore power, it is also a matter of economics.

Some friends returned recently from a month's cruise in the Chesapeake, and reported that the cheapest dockage they found anywhere was $1.25 a foot per night. With their 40-foot powerboat, that's $50 a night, without room service. The result was that they spent less than a week at a dock, and the rest of the time at anchor.

Docking does have its advantages. You can get on and off the boat easily, which is especially nice in bad weather. You can plug in, top up the tanks, and wash down the boat. I like to be dockside when we have a lot of laundry to do, or a lot of shopping. And if we are leaving the boat for quite a while, I feel better knowing she is tied securely to a dock.

Anchoring offers other pleasures, and to me anchoring out is more what cruising is all about than just going from dock to dock. At a dock, we are on the boat, but still tied to all the hustle and bustle of shore. At anchor, we're surrounded by water, and the sights and sounds are natural, not manmade. The feelings of independence, freedom, and yes, even romance, are very real and very enjoyable. Don't ask me why, but the sunsets are more beautiful at anchor than dockside.

ANCHORING

Anchoring out is only wonderful if you are prepared—if the boat is equipped with adequate ground tackle, if you have chosen the place to anchor with care, and if you know the anchor has dug in and the boat is secure. Then you can relax and enjoy your surroundings.

Ground Tackle

Proper anchoring starts with the boat and her equipment. Unfortunately, too many manufacturers still think of powerboats as going from marina to marina, and install an anchor platform suitable for only one anchor. This may be fine when you are just weekending and your anchoring is local, and generally in the same area week after week. A cruising boat, however, must carry two hefty anchors on deck (Figure 8-1), with room to stow another one elsewhere— usually aft.

There is no single anchor that will do the job in all weather conditions and in any type of bottom. When you are cruising, you may be anchoring in a different place almost every night, and carrying at least two different types of anchors will allow you to choose the best one for each particular situation. It's true that you will decide on a "favorite" anchor and use it most of the time, but you need another one for those other times, infrequent though they may be, and there will also be occasions when it is necessary to set two anchors.

FIGURE 8–1.   *This foredeck is set up for cruising, with two anchors—a CQR and a Bruce—carried in rollers on a sturdy anchoring platform, along with an electric windlass and plenty of working room.*

Types of Anchors

Everyone with a few cruising miles under their keel will have definite opinions about which anchor is best, and we all seem to swear by a different type. A C.Q.R. was our first choice for a long time, but after four years of cruising with a Bruce anchor it is now our primary anchor, with the C.Q.R. a close second. Our third anchor is a Danforth Hi-Tensile.

• DANFORTH ANCHOR

Danforth anchors have been around for a long time. They have excellent holding power for their weight, and they will lie flat so they are easier to stow on deck than other types. The new DeepSet Danforths have thinner flukes and shank and are supposed to have even greater holding power. Danforths work well in sand and mud, but not in grass, coral, rock, or clay. A Danforth will not always reset itself if the boat swings to a shift in wind or tide.

• C.Q.R. (PLOW) ANCHOR

This is a good all-around anchor, one that will hold well in almost all bottom conditions. The CQR will be larger (heavier) than a Danforth for the same size boat. Because of its shape and weight, it is impractical to keep it on deck and try to lift it over the side—it must be stowed in a bow roller. Once a C.Q.R. has dug in, its holding power is superb, and it will tend to stay put even when the boat swings.

• BRUCE ANCHOR

There doesn't seem to be any middle ground with Bruce anchors— folks either love them or hate them. I'm one who loves them. Like the CQR, a Bruce holds well in almost all bottom conditions, even rocks. I personally feel that a Bruce digs in faster, and holds better if the boat swings, than a CQR—but this is not based on any scientific study, simply my own experience. A Bruce is harder to stow than other types. It must be kept in a roller, or in a roller/mount designed specifically for it.

Anchor Size

This is always a hotly debated topic. While it's true that holding power depends on shape as well as weight, I still tend to lean toward "heavier is better." Table 8-1 offers suggestions for anchor sizes, based on the overall length of the boat. However, these are only suggestions. Many variables affect the size of anchor a boat needs— not just overall length but displacement, windage, draft, size of anchor rode, scope used, plus the worst weather and sea conditions you expect to encounter.

This last one is the hardest to predict, which is why I lean toward a larger anchor. You may plan your cruise for the time of year when the weather is best, but freak storms can happen and it's better to be prepared right from the start, rather than risk losing the boat because of inadequate ground tackle. According to the chart, our *Duchess* could carry a 33-pound Bruce anchor, which would be fine in almost all conditions. But she carries a 44-pound Bruce, the next size up, which in theory should hold her in as much as 60 knots of wind. I hope we never have to test that, although we have ridden out hurricane-force winds on other boats and made it through fine. It

Table 8-1
SUGGESTED SIZES (IN POUNDS) FOR WORKING ANCHOR

Boat Length	Danforth Deep/Set	Danforth Deep/Set Hi-Tensile	C.Q.R.	Bruce
24'-30'	10	9	25	11
31'-35'	15	9	35	16.5
36'-40'	18	12	35	22
41'-47'	31	12	45	33
48'-52'	48	17	45–60	44
52'-60'	48	—	60	66

Note: Storm anchor should be one size larger.

was not a pleasant experience, but a testament to both the boats and their anchoring gear.

Quite a few boats carry so-called "lunch hooks": small, light-weight anchors with perhaps a few feet of chain, to be used when anchoring for only a few hours—for lunch, or for a swim or dive. Other than for use with the dinghy, lunch hooks have no place on a cruising boat. If the boat is set up properly, with the working anchors in rollers and ready to go, and a good windlass to get the anchor back up, using the working anchor should be no more work than using a small one. You might decide to spend the night after all, or a summer squall could arrive without warning, causing a mad scramble that could have been easily avoided by using the right anchor in the first place.

Anchor Rode

Every anchor needs a length of chain, and the more the better. A rule of thumb used as a minimum by many cruisers is a length of chain equal to the length of the boat, and the rest of the rode is nylon line. The weight of the chain will act as a catenary between the boat and anchor and prevent violent surging in gusts of wind. The chain will keep the shank of the anchor down and provide a more horizontal pull, allowing the anchor to dig in better and stay put after it has dug in. An all-chain rode will cut down on the boat's swinging circle and allow you to use less scope—important considerations in a crowded anchorage. Also, chain is not subject to chafe and can lie across coral, rocks, or broken glass on the bottom without damage.

About the only disadvantage of an all-chain rode is the sheer weight of it all. Your windlass must be powerful enough to allow the smallest crewmember to handle the ground tackle with ease, and the boat must be large enough to take that much weight forward without affecting the trim or the way she handles.

Nylon rode has the ability to stretch, lessening the shock loads on boat and anchor. In my opinion, only three-strand nylon should be used. According to data from New England Ropes, at 15 percent of the rope's tensile strength, three-strand nylon will stretch 16.5 percent while nylon braid will stretch 6.5 percent—a difference of 10 percent. Dacron, of course, is noted for its *low* stretch. Braided line is more subject to chafe than three-strand, although any line used for anchoring should be protected—both by a length of chain to keep it off the bottom, and by wrapping it where it passes over the bow roller. It can be wrapped with a piece of leather, rags, a length of garden hose, just about anything that can be lashed to the rode will work, but it must have protection of some kind.

Since chain has no elasticity, a chain hook pendant (Figure 8-2) can be used with an all-chain rode. This is a length of nylon line with a hook, sized to fit the chain, attached to one end of the line. After the anchor has been set, the hook is inserted in one of the links and the other end of the pendant secured to a cleat. The chain is then payed out a bit so there is a loop of chain hanging between the hook and the end of the pendant, thus allowing the nylon to act as a shock absorber. A chain hook pendant isn't always necessary in calm weather, but in storm conditions it will greatly reduce the shock loads when the boat surges back and then fetches up violently on the anchor.

Whether the rode is all-chain, or a combination of chain and nylon line, 200 feet should be the minimum length for each anchor. Even better, use 250 feet to 300 feet of rode on at least the primary anchor. The shackle that attaches the chain to the anchor should be the type with a hole in the pin, so the pin can be wired in place and there's no chance of the shackle coming apart underwater.

Some people splice nylon line directly to the last chain link so it will run smoothly over the roller and down the pipe. There is some merit to this, particularly if you are using a windlass that incorporates a chain pipe designed for an all-chain rode. If you use a chain/rope combination, a shackle may not even fit down the pipe, and you will have to splice directly to the chain. However, when possible, I still

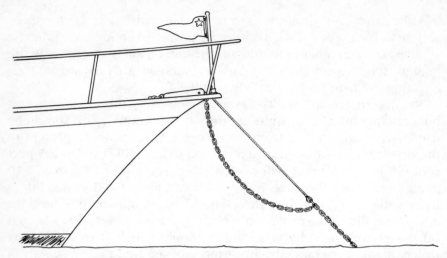

FIGURE 8–2. *A chain hook pendant acts as a shock absorber, lessening the surge when the boat pulls back on her anchor.*

prefer splicing the line around a thimble and attaching the thimble with a shackle. It allows you to make a larger eye splice and it is a stronger attachment.

On-Deck Washdowns

A pressure washdown system is a luxury bordering on necessity (Figure 8-3), especially when you are using a lot of chain. The bucket and brush routine is both slow and hard on the back. With a power windlass, you can step on the foot switch to haul the anchor while sluicing off mud and gunk with the pressure hose.

The pump for the washdown can be run off the batteries, the main engines, or the generator. Water can be drawn from a separate sea cock, or it can be teed off the engine's cooling water intake (provided it is large enough to handle the extra draw).

The Windlass

On cruising powerboats over 30 feet, an anchor windlass is a must. When you are using heavy anchors and plenty of chain, it is senseless to heave and sweat and risk back injury when you could do the job by simply stepping on a foot switch (or cranking by hand, if you have a manual windlass).

FIGURE 8–3. *An on-deck pressure washdown system eases the chore of cleaning the ground tackle as it comes up off the bottom. (Photo by Jill Lorenz)*

Most powerboats do have power windlasses, and most of them are built to withstand the marine environment, with enclosed motors mounted beneath the deck and out of the weather. Although they are, for the most part, very reliable, it's still a good idea to get one with a manual override so they are usable in any emergency.

The most common type is a 12-volt windlass, or 24-volt, depending on your electrical system. Although they gobble up power, the engines are invariably running while the anchor is being pulled, so electrical consumption is seldom a problem. For overload protection, a power windlass should always be fitted with its own circuit breaker.

The choice between a vertical windlass and a horizontal one is a matter of personal preference. A vertical capstan (Figure 8-4) takes up less deck space than a horizontal windlass, and line can be led to it from any direction. Most of them are designed to handle a chain/line anchor rode combination, as well as an all-chain rode.

A horizontal windlass (Figure 8-5) must be installed so the anchor rodes are led fairly to the chain gypsy and rope capstan. I prefer a horizontal windlass, because I find it easier to use when working with two anchors. *Duchess* has a two-speed Hercules M-1200 windlass, made by Muir Engineering, available from So-Pac in Seattle, Washington. It has a self-holding gear drive that allows the chain gypsy to be locked in place when the capstan is being used for the second anchor.

Anchoring Techniques

As anchorages become more crowded, anchoring techniques must change. It's no longer a case of picking the best spot, dropping the hook, and digging it in with the engine in reverse. You will still perform these tasks, of course, but how you approach them will be different in a crowd.

The best spot may already be occupied by a passel of boats. This could mean they are practicing the overworked herd instinct—how many times have you anchored in the perfect secluded spot, only to watch every boat coming in anchor right on top of you? It could also mean they are staying out of the way of commercial traffic, or seaplane landings, or avoiding a rock in the center of the harbor that's only visible at low tide. Careful study of the chart, as well as

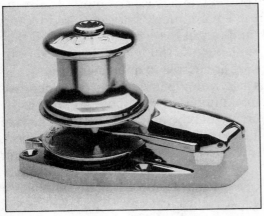

FIGURE 8–4. *A vertical windlass, like this Muir VRC 800, allows line to be led to it from any direction. The VRC 800 weighs 48 pounds and has a rated lift of 800 pounds. (Courtesy South Pacific Associates, Ltd.)*

FIGURE 8–5. *A horizontal windlass must be installed so the anchor rodes are led fairly to the gypsy and capstan. This Cougar model from Muir will operate on either 12 or 24-volts DC. At 55 pounds, it has a rated lift of 770 pounds. (Courtesy South Pacific Associates, Ltd.)*

any cruising guides, will give you a good idea of where you want to be long before you get there, but your own observations on arrival may change all those notions. The area may be littered with permanent moorings, or the wind may have changed direction, making a calm anchorage untenable. It's always a good idea to have a backup plan—other anchorages you selected before getting underway that morning—so if the first choice doesn't work out you have time to get to another place.

Anchoring in a crowd does pretty much force you to follow along. If all the boats are anchored on two anchors, you will have to do the same to restrict your swinging room unless you can get far enough away to set only one hook, and that is apt to put you in deeper water than you might like.

Setting anchor in a populated area frequently means anchoring with short scope. One of the great advantages of all-chain rode is that you can use as little as 3:1 scope in calm weather and still be secure. The old rule of thumb of 7:1 scope has little meaning in many of today's harbors—there just isn't enough room. The only solution is plenty of chain, if not all chain.

One anchoring technique that never changes is using hand signals whenever possible. Yelling back and forth from helm to foredeck will entertain the anchorage, but not necessarily your crew. If it is windy, or your engines especially noisy, it will be almost impossible to hear, anyway. Develop your own set of signals, and the whole job will go smoother and faster.

Some cruising folks like to set and retrieve the anchor from the bridge or pilot house, using a remote switch. A few companies, including So-Pac and Maxwell Marine, are now making electronic controls that provide both audible and visual overload warnings and incorporate an automatic shutdown feature. So-Pac's even has a digital readout of how many feet of rode have been let out, or brought in. I'm sure these are wonderful little tools, especially on a dark and stormy night when the last thing you want to do is venture up to the foredeck. However, I still feel that someone needs to be up there, especially in bad weather, to make sure all is going well. After the anchor has been dug in (by backing down with the engine in reverse), watch the line or chain, or put your foot on it—if it is vibrating it means the anchor is dragging. There is no way to check this from a remote location; you simply must be there, rain or shine.

Buoy and Trip Line

Setting the anchor with a buoy and trip line will help in several ways (Figure 8-6). If the anchor has fouled on a bottom obstruction, the trip line will allow you to capsize the anchor and pull it free. And the buoy will mark the spot where your anchor actually is in a crowded area, which hopefully will stop someone from dropping their anchor right on top of yours.

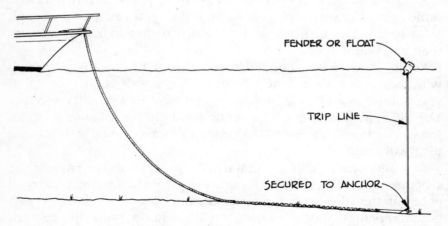

FIGURE 8–6.   *Rigging a trip line will help retrieve a fouled anchor as well as mark the spot where your anchor is located.*

Tie the trip line to the crown of the anchor, and tie a float to the other end. The float can be a fender, an empty Clorox bottle, or a small mooring buoy. It's a good idea to paint the name of your boat or the words "anchor buoy" on the float, to keep someone from rowing off with it. Be sure the trip line is long enough to allow the buoy to float easily, taking into account any rise in the tide.

Using Two Anchors

There are times when setting out a second anchor is a must. You may need the second anchor to reduce your swinging room—in a crowded anchorage, as already mentioned, or to stay off a beach or away from rocks if the wind should shift.

Anchoring bow-and-stern will keep the boat from swinging, but it only works if the boat is in line with any wind or current. If either is abeam, the boat's windage could easily cause her to drag. Setting two anchors off the bow is the better way.

A Bahamian moor, with two anchors set from the bow at about 180 degrees apart, is excellent when you must anchor in swift currents, since the boat will ride to one and then the other as the current changes direction (Figure 8-7). Since the boat will swing in her own length, the Bahamian moor is also good in tight quarters.

The anchors can also be set at a less severe angle, around 45 degrees. This is often done in storm conditions, so the boat is being held by both anchors at once. And if one should start to drag, the boat would likely fetch up on the other one and remain secure. The problem with setting anchors in this manner is that if the boat swings around, the two rodes twist together, and they must be untangled before weighing anchor.

The anchors can be set from the boat. Drop and set the first anchor, generally the upwind or upcurrent anchor. Then either allow the boat to drop back while letting out additional scope (twice the normal amount), or use the engines to power to the spot where you want to drop the second anchor. After the second anchor is set, you can take up on the rodes until the boat is centered between the two. Great care must be taken when doing this, particularly if you have a twin-screw boat, to make sure you don't run over one of the rodes or wrap it around a prop. It is often easier, and safer, to use the dinghy to row out the second anchor.

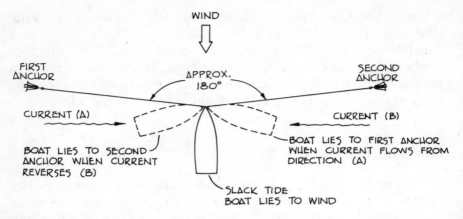

FIGURE 8–7.   *The Bahamian moor works well for anchoring in places with a swift current. It is also good for crowded anchorages with limited swinging room, since the boat will swing in her own length.*

Rocking and Rolling

Not all anchorages are idyllic places of calm serenity. Wind can come gusting down the face of a cliff, whipping the boat from side to side and making her fetch up on the anchor with a teeth-jarring jolt. A swell can curve around a headland, setting up a nasty chop that makes the boat dance and the crew queasy. If conditions are dangerous, the only solution is to get out, even if it means spending a night at sea. But if it's just uncomfortable, there are a few things that might help.

If your boat is a trawler type, with a mast and boom, a small steadying sail will help the boat lie head-to-wind and keep her from dancing around so much. Wally Chappin, owner of Oriental Sailmakers and representative for Hood Sails, says that since the sail is not used to drive the boat, it should be cut flat, and with a slight reverse curve to the sides to prevent flapping.

Flopper-stoppers will also reduce rolling. Refer back to The Comfort Factor chapter for a description of how these work, and their advantages and disadvantages.

Sometimes just moving to another part of the anchorage will make the boat more comfortable, by getting away from a tidal stream, or into the lee of protecting trees or buildings.

Anchoring Protocol

When we're lucky enough to find that rare bit of heaven—a completely deserted anchorage with no other boats, no sign of people on shore, just water, beach, and sky all to ourselves—then it can be a case of "anything goes." We can anchor where we choose, swim in the buff, make noise, do whatever we want. Within reason, of course. The responsibility remains to not dump garbage, litter beaches, take shells or fish in a restricted area, or do anything else to harm the environment, whether anyone is "watching" or not.

If there is another boat in the anchorage, however, or people ashore, then "anything" no longer goes and the courtesy that you extend to your neighbors at home applies to your neighbors afloat as well. A big point to remember is that sound travels across water like it never did across the back fence. Keep it in mind when you are dropping the hook, conversing over the noise of the outboard, playing a radio topside, or partying all night.

A cardinal rule in any anchorage is: The first boat to anchor has swinging rights. When you enter a crowded anchorage it is up to you to stay clear of everyone else, taking into account how they will lie if the wind shifts, and paying attention to whether they are on one anchor or two, and using all-chain or nylon rode. It will all make a difference in how, and where, you are able to anchor.

It's best to anchor astern of other boats. In fact, you can drop a hook right at another boat's transom, then drop back and remain well clear. If you anchor *ahead* of another boat, however, then you are likely to drop back and find yourself right on top of it, giving the owner a reason to worry all night about the chance that you might drag. You might think you are well clear, only to discover when the wind pipes up that your chain has straightened out and your transom is on the other boat's foredeck. This always happens in the middle of the night and pleasantries are seldom exchanged.

DOCKING

Chances are, by the time you set off for a cruise, you have gained considerable experience in handling your boat—from short weekend trips, perhaps, or just evening outings after a long day at work.

Most of us get pretty good at coming and going at our own dock. The surroundings are familiar, we adjust to the vagaries of local weather, we learn to deal with local tides and currents.

When we leave home waters, however, things can be a lot different. We may be used to little or no tide, and find ourselves at a fixed dock with a nine-foot tidal range. Dealing with swift currents may be a new experience, and slips may be narrower or marinas more congested than the one back home. It can all be part of the adventure, but it pays to understand how your boat behaves before taking off.

Docking Gear

It doesn't take a lot of gear to secure the boat properly, but it all should be of first quality and inspected frequently for signs of chafe or wear.

• MOORING LINES

Like anchor line, I believe that mooring lines should be of three-strand nylon. The nylon has enough stretch to act as a shock absorber, reducing strains on the boat and her fittings when wind or current is causing her to pull and tug at her lines.

A rule of thumb is that mooring lines should be as long as the boat, as a minimum. It's a good idea to have at least a pair of them that are longer, especially if your cruising plans include going through locks, where lines are generally doubled around a bollard on shore and the length must allow for the rise or fall of the water in the lock. If you have six dock lines, each with a large eye splice in one end, you will find that there are occasions when you are using them all.

• FENDERS AND FENDER BOARDS

Four to six fenders are a must. The time will come when you need to fender the boat on both sides, not just against a dock. The larger the diameter of the fender, the more protection it will give.

No cruising boat should be without a fender board (Figure 8-8). They are most often simply a length of standard two-by-four, with rubber end caps (sold in most marine stores) and holes drilled to receive the lines. A fender board is the only thing that will work if you are secured to a dock that has the pilings *outside* of the planking. If

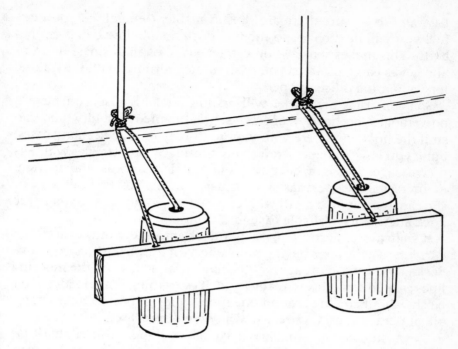

FIGURE 8–8.   *A fender board will distribute the shock loads and take more abuse than fenders alone.*

there is a surge running in the marina, the fender board will distribute the shock loads and take more abuse than fenders alone would.

• **CHAFE GEAR**

If wind or waves are causing the boat to bounce around, mooring lines can show signs of wear in a surprisingly short time. Chafe gear, similar to that used for anchor rode, is a must. And snubbers used with the lines will both reduce chafe and lessen shock loads on the boat and her deck fittings.

Docking Techniques

Docking at a new marina can sometimes be a trying experience, but taking it slow and planning ahead can usually minimize the stress.

Always call ahead if possible, to let the dockmaster know your

ETA and to be sure there are slips available. Generally if you need fuel you will be directed to the fuel dock first, before being given a berth. This makes sense—you can take care of all business up front and get as early a start as you wish in the morning, without waiting for the marina office to open.

Some marina personnel will assume that because you have a powerboat, you have twin screws, great maneuverability, and can stuff the boat anywhere you want to. It may be true in many cases, but if you have a single-screw, heavy-displacement trawler with lots of windage that is a bear to handle at low speeds and in tight quarters, tell the dockmaster the situation when you first call so he or she can assign you a berth with easy access—or make sure there are dock attendants available to lend a hand.

It's always easier to approach a dock into the wind, or into the current, whichever is having more effect on the boat. Once you have decided on your approach, get the fenders attached and the mooring lines cleated, coiled, and ready to go. If everything is not ready, don't be shy about circling around one more time—it beats a mad scramble or dented topsides because you weren't prepared.

Spring lines are invaluable when docking, especially in tight situations. Spring lines will stop the fore and aft movement of the boat, and they can be used as a pivot point to swing the bow or stern into, or away from, the dock. A spring line is generally the first line secured, and the last one cast off.

If there is no one on the dock to help when casting off, run the last spring line in a continuous loop around a cleat or piling, so it can be eased off from aboard ship and pulled free as you get underway.

Bow Thrusters

Bow thrusters (Figure 8-9), once the domain of commercial craft and megayachts, are now showing up on smaller and smaller pleasure boats. They can give an unwieldy single-screw cruiser the same maneuverability as a twin-screw boat.

Basically, a bow thruster is a propeller (or pair of propellers), installed in a tube through the bow of the boat, that provides enough force to push the bow of the boat sideways. They can be powered by either electricity or hydraulics, although the electric ones don't have enough power to be of real value on anything but small yachts.

FIGURE 8–9. *A bow thruster is a propeller (or pair of propellers), installed in a tube through the bow of the boat as shown here, that provides enough force to push the bow of the boat sideways.*

Bow thrusters are great for docking, but they can also be used to hold the bow into the wind when dropping the anchor, to keep the boat in position in the turbulence of a lock, and to get away when wind or current has the boat pinned against a pier.

Marina Protocol

When you think about it, staying in even the poshest marina borders on slum conditions. Yes, really—there are only a couple of feet of dock separating you from your neighbor, and you can look in their windows as easily as they can look in yours. The dock-walking public always assumes that docked boats are there for their perusal and entertainment. Privacy in a marina is zip. If you decide to shower ashore instead of onboard, the facilities may or may not be clean, and chances are you'll have to wait your turn.

What this means is that the common courtesies you extended to your neighbors at home must apply tenfold to your neighbors in a marina. Most find this is easy—easier than at home actually—because we are relaxed, enjoying ourselves, and generally have more in common with the cruising folks on the next boat than we did with the folks in the house next door.

The same courtesy should also apply to the dockmaster and other marina workers, but unfortunately this is not always the case. Too often I've seen them treated like servants, which results in slow and surly service. If you treat them with respect, and can handle delays or problems with a sense of humor, you may be surprised at just how helpful they can be. Marina operators are generally a great source of local knowledge and can pass along all sorts of information—about local weather and sea conditions, tips about good fishing or dive spots, as well as where to shop and dine ashore.

Although most yacht clubs still extend reciprocal privileges, it is becoming increasingly rare to find that they actually offer dockage. There are simply more boats out cruising than there are docks to berth them. You will probably find a friendly bar, a dinghy dock, a clean shower, a place to dump your trash, and maybe a good meal; but if you also manage to get a slip, consider yourself lucky.

Whether anchoring out or securing alongside a dock, deciding where to stay for the night, or for a week, is all part of the adventure. It means seeing new places and meeting new people. Whether the adventure brings pleasure or stress has everything to do with preparation. If the boat has adequate ground tackle, sufficient mooring lines and fenders, and you and the crew are confident in your abilities to handle the boat and her gear, then the adventures will be fun and stress will be something you left behind.

CHAPTER 9

Navigation

ELECTRONICS ARE CONSTANTLY being changed and updated. Last year's model is old hat this year, replaced by one with more functions, more buttons, more goodies. We won't even try to cover all the specific types or brands of electronic equipment in great detail here, because they do change so fast, plus there are a number of books available devoted entirely to the subject. What does not change, however, is the art of navigation itself. We still must get from point A to point B, in a safe and seamanlike manner. And while nothing can replace our own eyes and ears, our own knowledge and abilities for dead reckoning, reading the water, watching the weather, or following a compass course, electronics can make it all a whole lot easier. Trawler-type powerboats in particular seem to have spacious, well-planned pilot houses (Figure 9-1), with room to arrange a myriad of electronics where everything is easily read and handy to the helm.

MARINE RADIOS

Marine radios can keep us in touch with the rest of the world, no matter where we are. They can provide contact with other boats and

FIGURE 9–1.   *The Krogen 42* Joan M *has a spacious, well-planned pilot house, with plenty of working room for electronics and instruments—all easily accessible.*

with shore, as well as emergency communications and vital weather reports.

VHF Radio

VHF (very high frequency) radio (Figure 9-2) is found on just about every boat afloat today. In one respect, this commonality is bad. Far too many boat owners use VHF just like they use CB ashore. Try to call ahead to a marina on a summer afternoon in a busy area, and you'll find the airways cluttered with "good buddies" chatting away as though Channel 16 was their own private telephone line.

The FCC does have rules governing the use of VHF; and using CB jargon is, in fact, illegal. It is also illegal to call the Coast Guard for a radio check, or to use the radio for social calls. We all know how much attention is paid to these rules, but nevertheless they are rules. The exception to not using a VHF for social or personal reasons is ship-to-shore calls placed through the Marine Operator—these can be of a personal nature.

Channel 16 is the international distress, safety, and calling chan-

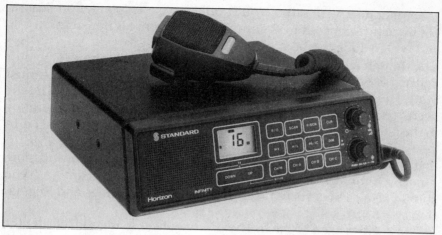

FIGURE 9–2. *A VHF radio, like this Horizon International model, is standard equipment on just about every boat afloat today. (Courtesy Standard Communications Corporation)*

nel. It must be monitored whenever you have the radio on and are not using another channel. Other than distress or safety calls, 16 is used to establish contact with another ship before switching to a working channel. The chart in Table 9-1 lists the VHF channels generally used by pleasure boats.

Table 9-1
VHF CHANNELS FOR PLEASURE BOATS

Channel	Used for
16	Distress, safety, and calling. A required channel.
06	Intership safety. A required channel.
22A	Communications with U.S. Coast Guard.
1, 5, 12, 14, 20, 63, 73, 74, 77	Port operations, traffic advisory. Intership and ship to shore.
13, 67	Navigational. Intership and ship to shore. 13 is commonly used by bridge tenders.
9, 68, 69, 71, 72	Non-commercial. Intership and ship to shore.
70, 72	Non-commercial. Intership.
24, 25, 26, 27, 28, 84, 85, 86, 87	Public communication—marine operator. Ship to shore.
WX-1, WX-2, WX-3	NOAA weather broadcasts.

To operate a VHF radio, you should have a ship's station license, obtained by filling out FCC Form 506. The license is non-transferable and will include the boat's call sign.

Although a personal license (Restricted Radiotelephone Operator Permit) is no longer required for most domestic calls in the United States, it is required if you use your VHF in other countries. And the license is also required for radio users on boats over 65 feet operating in the Great Lakes. There is no test for this license, but you must be 14 years of age or older. It is obtained by filling out FCC Form 753.

It is no longer necessary to keep a log of every radio transmission, but you should record any distress calls that you hear. And you should also carry a current copy of the FCC VHF Rules and Regulations.

The licenses are $35 each. The personal license is good for life; the ship's station license must be renewed every five years. You can get the forms by writing to:

Federal Communications Commission
Marine Ship Service
P.O. Box 358275
Pittsburgh, PA 15251-5275

The rules and regulations are available in simplified form in a booklet called "How to Use Your VHF Marine Radio: FCC Rules for Recreational Boaters, Part 83, Subpart CC." It can be ordered for $3.75 from:

Superintendent of Documents
U.S. Government Printing Office
Washington, D.C. 20402

Ship-to-shore calls made through the marine operator can sometimes be billed to your home or business phone, your telephone credit card, and sometimes the call can be made collect—the procedures vary from one area to the next. The easiest way to handle the billing is with a MIN card—this is a credit card with a marine identification number. You can get one through your telephone company's mobile marine division. There is no fee for the card, you are only billed when a call is made, and the card is valid anywhere in the U.S. and in parts of Canada.

VHF radio waves are line-of-sight; that is, they do not bend to follow the curve of the earth, so your operating range is determined by the height of your antenna. Generally, you can expect ship-to-ship communication of around 20 miles, and 50 miles or better with Coast Guard shore stations and marine operators since their antennas are relatively high.

Single Sideband (SSB) Radio

Marine SSB radios (Figure 9-3) operate on medium and high frequencies. While VHF provides communication over short distances, SSB allows long-distance communication of ship-to-ship and ship-to-shore. How long a distance depends on many variables, such as time of day and which frequencies are used.

By law a VHF radio must be installed in a boat before single sideband, or any other radio, can be added. And you cannot place calls through single sideband as long as you are within range of VHF. So unless your cruising will take you far enough offshore to be out of VHF range, the SSB is likely to be little more than an expensive listening device. However, when we were cruising in the southern

FIGURE 9–3.   *A marine SSB radio, like this IC-725 all-band transceiver, allows long-distance communications beyond the range of VHF. (Courtesy ICOM Inc.)*

Bahamas, we found that the only reliable weather forecast we could get was on our SSB radio. We used the VHF for communications, but could not get the weather channels.

Installing SSB is not a simple matter. It requires an elaborate ground-plate system, special antenna, and generally an antenna tuner as well. The VHF station license can be used for SSB, although it may have to be upgraded to include the SSB frequencies. And a personal operator's license is required for SSB.

There are four coastal stations in the United States that handle high-seas radiotelephone traffic. If you think you will be making a lot of calls, you can register with one or all of them, depending on your cruising range, and your calls will automatically be billed to your home or office. Three of the stations—KMI in Point Reyes, California, WOM in Fort Lauderdale, Florida, and WOO in Manahawkin, New Jersey—are operated by AT&T. You can register by calling 1-800-SEA-CALL. The fourth station is WLO, Mobile Marine Radio, Inc., 7700 Rinla Ave., Mobile, Alabama 36619.

If you call AT&T, be sure to request their informative booklet "AT&T High Seas Radio Service—Fingertip Guide." Another good book on radio procedures is the "Marine Radiotelephone Users Handbook," available for $7.95 from:

RTCM
P.O. Box 19087
Washington, DC 20036

Amateur (ham) SSB radio operates on different frequencies than marine SSB. Unlike VHF or marine SSB, you must pass tests—both theory and Morse code—before you can use these frequencies. Absolutely no business can be conducted on the amateur bands—they are strictly for personal communications. There are many maritime mobile "nets," both along the coast and throughout the world. These are ham operators who get together on the radio at designated times and exchange cruising information, weather reports, messages from other cruisers or folks back home, and generally keep tabs on each other.

If you are interested in getting a ham license, write to:

American Radio Relay League
225 Main Street
Newington, CT 06111

INSTRUMENTATION

Choosing the instrumentation for a cruising boat can be fun, but it can also be frustrating simply because of the sheer number of instruments to choose from. Probably the best place to shop is a boat show, but just talk to salespeople and pick up brochures, then go back to your boat and decide what you *really* need.

Many companies now offer models that combine several functions in one unit. Ray Jefferson's Model 250 computer, for example, combines ten functions in one small package: instant speed, average speed, acceleration, cumulative log, trip distance, log trip time, 24-hour clock, clock alarm, stopwatch, and countdown time display. While it is a space-saver, the real question must be how many of the functions you would actually use. The stopwatch and countdown time would be useful only if you like running predicted log races or serve as a committee boat for sailboat races. On a pure cruising boat, they would be pointless.

I personally like to be able to read my instruments at a glance, without having to punch a keypad to bring up each function. This does not rule out multi-function instruments, however. Datamarine's Dart Model 2490 is fairly typical of multi-function instruments that display several functions simultaneously. It shows depth, boat speed, average speed, temperature, and distance log, and includes depth alarms as well. The unit shows depths to 500 feet and speeds to 60 mph with a transom transducer, or to 40 mph with a through-hull transducer.

You can install instrumentation that is as simple, or as sophisticated, as you like. You'll find instruments that will interface with your Loran or Sat-Nav and display compass heading, degrees and direction off-course, or compute your ETA. And all sorts of alarms are available—everything from burglar and fire alarms to fume and high-water detectors to anchor-dragging and shallow-water alarms. Name a potential problem and I'll bet you can find an alarm for it.

DEPTH SOUNDERS

A depth sounder is a must on a cruising boat. I've always been satisfied with a digital readout instrument, but many cruisers (including my husband) prefer a flashing unit. They do have the advantage of supplying an overall "picture" of the bottom plus giving you an idea of the type of bottom. For example, a wide-bottom flash most likely means a mud or grassy bottom, while a narrow flash would indicate a hard bottom—rock or sand.

Recording depth sounders are excellent for navigating along a coastline, by enabling you to follow charted contour lines along the bottom. This can be a great help if you are unsure of your position or inching your way along in fog. A flasher depth sounder can also be used for this, although it is easier with a recorder.

I guess my only reason for preferring a digital depth sounder is that I find them much easier to read at a glance. They are fine for giving the depth when anchoring, or a warning when you are getting into shallow water; they are just not very good for navigating purposes.

LORAN

Loran is an excellent aid to navigation for coastal and Great Lakes cruising (Figure 9-4). If you are heading south on either coast—Mexico or the Bahamas—coverage will deteriorate the farther south you go. We were able to get good fixes in the northern Bahamas, but past Nassau our Loran was useless.

Loran provides accurate position fixes by measuring the time difference (TD) between transmissions from a master station and one or more secondary stations. Initial accuracy (finding a place for the first time) is generally around a quarter of a mile. But one of the great features of Loran is that you can enter your own fixes, or "waypoints," and later return to within 50 feet of that point. For example, you can enter the waypoint of a harbor entrance buoy, or the place where you had to cut loose an anchor, and return to the buoy in the fog or to retrieve the anchor when the weather has calmed.

A Loran antenna is a whip antenna much like a CB antenna. Height does not matter when mounting the antenna, but it should be placed as far as possible from a VHF or SSB antenna.

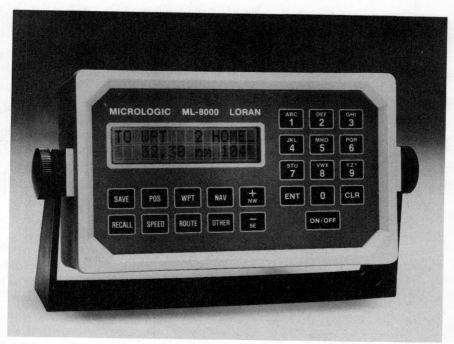

FIGURE 9–4.   *Loran provides a position fix by measuring the time difference between transmissions from two or more stations. (Courtesy Micrologic)*

SATELLITE NAVIGATION

Satellite Navigation (SatNav) will provide extremely accurate position fixes anywhere in the world. Unlike Loran, which will give fixes continuously, SatNav gives an updated fix on each pass of a satellite. The frequency of passes varies, depending on your location, but in most places you can generally count on a pass at least once every hour.

Current equipment operates with the U.S. Transit Satellite System. This system will be in operation until at least 1995, and probably beyond. It will eventually be phased out by the Global Positioning System (GPS). As of April 1988, half of the projected 18 GPS satellites were in orbit, and seven of them were operational. The present schedule calls for the system to be complete by 1991.

There are manufacturers, such as Furuno and Magnavox, who are already building equipment capable of tracking both Transit and the GPS that is available today. All of the Magnavox MX 1100 series is capable of being upgraded to accept future GPS by adding or exchanging printed circuit boards. It's a feature worth looking for if you are in the market today for a SatNav.

SatNav is not cheap. You'll be paying several thousand dollars, compared to several hundred for Loran. Whether or not you can justify the expense will depend on your style of cruising. If you are heading offshore for long-distance voyaging, then you may find SatNav indispensable; but most coastal cruisers are satisfied with Loran or an RDF.

Radar

Radar can be a tremendous aid, particularly when you are navigating along a shoreline at night or in bad weather. In pea-soup fog, or on a dark, moonless night, radar will allow you to "see" the shoreline, buoys, other boats, all sorts of dangers that might be missed with limited visibility.

Rather than the old-style cathode-ray tube display unit, you can now get display screens much like a TV screen or a computer monitor (Figure 9-5). These raster scan radars have the advantage of being easy to view in daylight without using a hood like the old types, plus the monitor can sometimes be used for other functions as well.

Radar waves, like VHF, are line of sight, so the higher the antenna can be mounted, the better. Since the antenna unit includes the transmitter and receiver, it is heavy—anywhere from 25 to 50 pounds—and must be mounted securely where it won't get damaged or torn loose in a seaway.

I've seen some powerboats with the radar antenna mounted on a pilot house top, which is fine unless there is a flying bridge that places people above or in line with the antenna. When the unit is in operation, radiation is being emitted and it is foolish to take chances, no matter how small a "dose" you might be getting. Place the antenna *above* anyplace where someone might be standing.

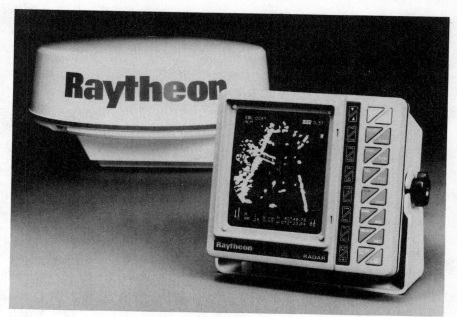

FIGURE 9—5.   *Raster scan radar, like this Raytheon R10 model, are easy to view in daylight without using a hood like the old-style radars. (Courtesy Raytheon Marine Company)*

RADIO DIRECTION FINDER

With all the fancy electronics available today, a radio direction finder (RDF) may seem outdated, but in fact it is still a very viable navigation aid. Anywhere along the coast, including southern latitudes where Loran may not be any good, radio beacon stations can provide position fixes—and at a fraction of the cost of SatNav.

Marine radio beacons are broadcast on frequencies located below the AM bands, and both the radio beacons and sometimes AM stations as well can be used for fixes or to home into a harbor. Beacons can originate from lighthouses, harbor buoys, jetty entrances, as well as from individual radio towers. Check your chart for the location of marine beacons. They are also listed in the Coast Guard *Light Lists*, available from the Superintendent of Documents; or in *Radio Navigational Aids*, documents 117A and 117B, published by the Defense Mapping Agency. These can be purchased from:

DMA Office of Distribution Services
6500 Brookes Lane
Washington, DC 20315

WEATHER FACSIMILE

If you don't have a lot of confidence in NOAA weather reports, or if your cruising will take you to areas where weather reports are hard to get, then a weather facsimile recorder (Figure 11-1) may be the answer.

A weatherfax will print out weather and oceanographic charts on a daily basis, allowing you to track storms, locate fronts, and generally predict the weather for yourself. However, unless you are already a meteorologist, it will take some time and study to learn how to interpret and use the wealth of information a weatherfax can provide.

Weather facsimile recorders can be purchased as individual units, or you can buy just a recorder, such as the Faxmate from Alden Electronics, that will work with an SSB or ham radio that carries the radiofax frequencies. The Faxmate can also be used as a printer for an onboard computer.

AUTOPILOTS

An autopilot can be one of the most worthwhile additions you can make to a cruising powerboat. It will do the sometimes tedious work of steering while you dash to the galley for a cup of coffee, plot a course on the chart, watch the radar screen, or stroll forward with the binoculars to look for a buoy. It can only do what it is told, however, and can never take the place of a pair of eyes to watch for other boats, buoys, or reefs. More than one boat has been lost because the owner set a course, flipped a switch, and went below to party or nap while his trusty autopilot took the boat right up on the beach.

Most autopilots today are small computers that can be programmed to make adjustments for trim and sea conditions as well as steer a compass course. Most autopilots can also interface with Sat-Nav or Loran. This can be particularly valuable since the Loran will be keeping track of your position and can make adjustments for any offsetting effects of wind or current, which the autopilot alone cannot do—it will simply hold to the course until it's told otherwise.

Autopilots are expensive. Plan on spending anywhere from $2,500 up to $6,000, depending on how sophisticated a unit you want. It's a lot of money, but if you plan on a lot of cruising miles, an autopilot will pay for itself many times over.

THE ART OF NAVIGATION

Electronics can provide us with a tremendous amount of information, but it is up to us to make the decisions that put that information to use. The radar can show us a jetty at a harbor entrance, a Loran waypoint can tell us when we are approaching a marker buoy, but whether to run the entrance or wait until the fog lifts is a decision that we, and not the gear, must make.

And electronics aside, there is much information available just through our own powers of observation—cloud formations can warn of an approaching thunderstorm, water marks on pilings or rocks can tell the state of the tide, eddies around buoys can indicate direction and speed of current, and the color of the water can suggest depth and bottom condition.

Tides and Currents

Both tides and currents will have a significant effect on navigation. Knowing both the range of tide and the time of high and low water will determine how much scope to let out when anchoring, how to secure the boat to a fixed dock, and if and when it is safe to cross a shoal or clear a bridge.

Currents can have an even greater effect. They can make a difference in speed over the bottom, fuel economy, and the safety of the ship itself. Powerboats generally have enough power to stay under control and make headway against swift current, although I still remember being part of a delivery crew on a 50-foot trawler that could barely maintain headway against a raging current in the Strait of Juan de Fuca between Vancouver Island and Washington.

Whether it's the Strait of Juan de Fuca, the East River in New York, the Chesapeake and Delaware Canal, or any other area noted for tricky currents, careful study of current charts and tables can help you time your passage for the easiest and safest run. Whether the current is with you or against you, if it is running hard it can create rips and eddies that can make boat-handling difficult. Wind against tide can cause a nasty chop. Running as much of a passage as possible with slack tide is generally the best practice.

Navigating in Fog

While the best policy for dealing with fog (or heavy rain—anything that reduces visibility) is to stay in port, it's not always possible. Radar comes into its own in heavy weather, but it is still no substitute for posting a lookout.

The best place for a lookout is right up in the bow, and they are there to *listen* as much as they are there to look. Engines should be slowed to idle, just enough to maintain steerage, and it's not a bad idea to shut them down periodically so you really hear what is around you. Sound may be your only warning of approaching danger. Whether it is the sound of another boat, a bell buoy, surf on a beach, or seals on rocks, you won't hear any of it if the engines are roaring at full speed ahead.

Ship traffic can be a real concern in foggy weather, since ships don't always reduce speed and they may or may not pick you up on their radar. They will, however, stay in designated shipping lanes and it is often possible for yachts to travel outside the lanes and still be in deep water.

Reading the Water

We are all used to judging water depth by simply glancing at the depth sounder. The only drawback to this is that it tells us the depth of water the boat is already in, and it may be telling us what we already know—the boat is aground.

If the water is clear, you can learn to judge depth by the color of the water. I first learned to do this in the Bahamas; with just a little practice it becomes quite easy.

The higher you can get above the water, the easier it is to do. A flying bridge is the best spot, right up in the bow is the second best.

The sun should be high and behind you. A cloudy day, or when the sun is low (early morning, late evening), will make it difficult if not impossible to read the water. Polarized sunglasses can help.

Dark-blue or dark-green water is usually deep enough for passage. The color will lighten as the water shoals. Pale green becoming white means you are just about aground. Dark patches can mean rocks or coral, or patches of grass. A coral head is sometimes surrounded by a ring of white sand. It's best to just avoid all dark patches. Interpreting shading from dark to light, and learning to tell rocks from grass, takes practice, but you'll be surprised at how fast you pick it up.

Obstructions

Sharing the waterways with commercial fishermen can add a real challenge to safe navigation. You might expect that they would set their crab and lobster pots and fish traps *outside* of busy channels, but it doesn't work that way. I try to be nice about this—after all, they are trying to make a living and I am just there for fun—but I have seen markers so thick that it was just about impossible to work through or around them.

A single screw boat, with the propeller protected by skeg and rudder, can usually hit a buoy and it will just bounce along the side and float harmlessly away in the boat's wake. A twin screw is likely to wrap the line around an exposed prop. If this happens, try to get it off without cutting the line if it's possible.

Navigation is a big part of cruising, and most of us find it a very enjoyable part. Whether we enjoy using all the available electronics, or just chart, compass, and depth sounder, navigating a boat is so much more interesting and more of a challenge than reading a road map and driving a car down a highway. The most important ingredient is common sense, followed closely by good planning. Take the time to study the charts, the guidebooks, the tide tables. Plan the day's run before you leave the dock or pull the anchor, and you'll find the passage goes smoother and you are better prepared to deal with any problems or emergencies that might arise.

CHAPTER 10

Seamanship

SEAMANSHIP IS A BROAD TERM, covering a multitude of skills and a host of knowledge. It includes boat-handling abilities, piloting skills, a knowledge of the rules of the road, and the experience and judgment to deal with emergencies when they arise.

RULES OF THE ROAD

Everyone who ventures out on the water should have a working knowledge of the rules of the road. If you are offshore with no sign of another boat for miles around, then your knowledge, or lack of it, probably won't matter a lot. But inshore, where most of us spend the majority of our cruising time, it can be critical. There is only so much navigable water, but the number of boats using that water is increasing daily. Fishing boats, tugs and barges, tankers, cruisers, runabouts, sailboats, and windsurfers—everyone is out there, everyone has their rights, and unfortunately not everyone knows what they are.

I'm always surprised by how many people still think that a sailboat, under sail, has the right of way over everyone else. Not true! Although this is an oversimplification, generally the least maneuverable boat has the right of way. The following list ranks boats according to who has right of way over the rest, starting with the "most privileged":

1. Vessels not under command (a powerboat whose engine just quit, for example).
2. Vessels with restricted maneuvering ability (such as a large ship in a narrow channel).
3. Vessels engaged in commercial fishing (this does not apply to sport fishing).
4. Vessels under sail (with no auxiliary power).
5. Vessels under power (including sailboats using their engines).

A tanker navigating a narrow channel won't be able to get out of anyone's way, or to stop quickly. The same is true for a tug pushing or pulling a string of unwieldy barges. Rules of the road aside, common sense dictates that we stay out of their way.

The rules of the road include regulations covering right of way, sound signals, navigation lights and shapes, and emergency signals. They are spelled out in the softcover book *Navigation Rules— International and Inland.* It is available at many chandleries, or for $7.50 from the Superintendent of Documents, U.S. Government Printing Office, Washington, D.C. 20402.

All boats that are 12 meters (39.4 feet) or longer are required to carry a copy aboard, but every cruising boat, regardless of length, should have a copy. And every boat owner should read and understand the rules. If you have trouble remembering some of the rules that you must use frequently, write them down and post them near the helm. For instance, if you are cruising a waterway with a lot of barge traffic and whistle signals are common, write the signals on a 3-by-5 card:

1 blast—"I am altering course to starboard."
2 blasts—"I am altering course to port."
3 blasts—"My engines are operating astern."
5 blasts—the danger signal.

Then tack up the card where it is visible to the helm. Even if you remember all the signals, it may help a crew member or a guest who is taking a turn at steering and may not be as familiar as you are with the rules. In close encounters, there is seldom time to find the book and look up the proper signal. Whoever is on the helm must be able to both understand signals and respond promptly.

PASSING AND BEING PASSED

I think I have seen more frayed tempers, more nasty words exchanged because of passing techniques than any other situation on the water. The procedure is really quite simple, but it does require cooperation from both boats, not just one.

The secret is for *both* boats to slow down. If a boat is traveling at six or seven knots, then an overtaking boat must pass at eight or ten knots, which is bound to leave the slow boat bouncing and rolling in the wake.

The boat being passed should slow down as much as possible while still maintaining steerage. This will allow the overtaking boat to reduce speed to just a couple of knots as soon as it is abeam, leaving little wake. If the overtaking boat refuses to slow down, her skipper deserves to be keelhauled.

If you happen to be the overtaken boat, you can minimize the rolling by turning directly into the passing boat's wake as soon as you safely can, taking the brunt of it head-on. Then turn quickly into the center part of the wake, where the water is flat, and follow right astern until the channel has calmed (Figure 10-1).

The rules of the road are very specific about passing, and they should be studied carefully, but in brief they cover three situations—meeting, crossing, and overtaking.

• Meeting—when two boats under power are meeting head-on, neither has the right of way. They should pass port to port; both should alter course to starboard to avoid collision (Figure 10-2). Anytime you make a course change, make it big and obvious so the other boat will understand your intentions. Slight course corrections are unlikely to even be noticed.

- Crossing—the boat to starboard normally has right of way, and the boat to port must change course or speed to avoid collision (Figure 10-3). There are exceptions to this, which is why the rules deserve careful study.
- Overtaking—the boat being overtaken is "privileged" and must maintain course and speed. The overtaking boat is the "burdened" vessel and must stay clear at all times.

WATCH YOUR WAKE

Even if there is not another boat in sight, you should still pay attention to your wake, and keep in mind that you are legally responsible for any damage caused by your wake.

In the narrow channels and landcuts along the Intracoastal Waterway, trees falling into the water are a common sight, their root systems destroyed as the soil beneath them is cut away by passing boat wakes. Untold damage is done each year to the land, and the bulkheads, docks and pilings of homeowners along the waterway. Some of these folks have become irate enough to take an occasional shot at a passing speedboat.

This is admittedly sometimes a Catch 22. Some planing boats leave a tremendous wake at slow—less than planing—speeds. Yet many waterways are posted with speed limits, generally 5 knots maximum, and that is "wake speed" for many hulls.

There are really only two solutions. Either slow down to no-wake speed, adapting a "what's the rush anyway" attitude; or head for open water where you can crank it up and run the boat at her designed performance speed, leaving the peaceful waterways peaceful, and intact.

COMMERCIAL TRAFFIC

We've already established that those of us cruising in powerboats are at the bottom of the right-of-way totem pole. That's fine with me. Our boats are, generally, among the most maneuverable on the water, and we are out there for pleasure, not for our livelihood. Commercial boats expect us to stay out of the way, and rightly so.

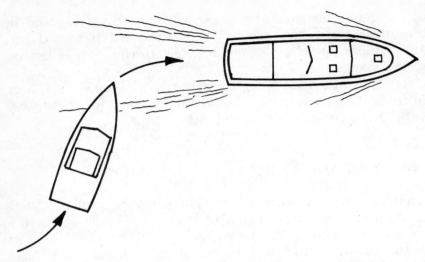

FIGURE 10–1.   *After being passed, you can minimize the rolling by turning directly into the passing boat's wake and then turning quickly into the smooth, center part of the wake.*

This does not mean they will run us down if we're in the wrong place at the wrong time. On the contrary, I have found skippers of commercial craft to be among the most helpful, and the most knowledgeable, seamen around. Towboat captains are particularly skillful, pushing or pulling a string of barges that may exceed 1,000 feet in length.

Passing such a rig can be a nervous proposition, and your best bet is to call the tug's captain on VHF. Although normal procedure is to place a call on channel 16 and then switch to a working channel, I've found that if I can't make contact on 16, I can usually get a quick response by initiating the call on channel 13. Ask if it is safe to pass and on which side you should pass. They are likely to tell you to "pass on two whistles" or "pass on one whistle," so you had better know your signals.

Commercial fishing boats should always be given a wide berth, particularly ones that are trawling. The nets are deep and wide, and when they are down the ship can only make slow, sweeping turns. You don't want to get in their way, and you certainly don't want to get a net wrapped around a prop.

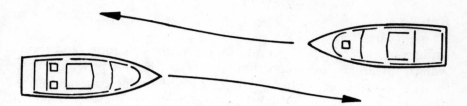

FIGURE 10–2. *Two boats meeting head-on should both turn to starboard and pass each other port to port.*

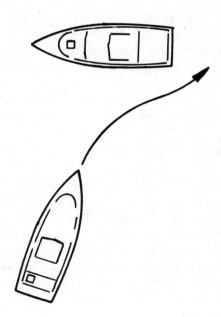

FIGURE 10–3. *When two boats are converging, the boat to port must change course or speed to avoid collision.*

BRIDGES

Bridges are ever-present on any inland cruise. As more and more waterfront land is developed, more bridges are built to provide access to what were once secluded islands. Fixed bridges are seldom a problem—you can either make it or you can't, or you wait for a low tide.

Opening bridges, on the other hand, can add a little spice to the cruise. As waterway traffic increases, it is becoming quite common for bridges to open on a schedule, rather than on demand. Depending on the speed of your boat, it may be possible to calculate time and distance and adjust your speed to make each bridge opening without having a long wait.

It is important to know the height of your boat. You may be able to clear many bridges without asking for an opening. Remember, too, that you are required to lower anything that *can* be lowered— outriggers, antennas, biminis—if lowering it means you can clear. If you are too lazy to lower an antenna, the bridge tender does not have to open.

The signal for requesting an opening is one long blast followed by one short blast. It is usually better to call the bridge tender on VHF. Like tug captains, bridge tenders usually respond on channel 16 but sometimes only on 13. Calling ahead is particularly helpful if the bridge is close ahead but out of sight around a bend. If a tender knows that several boats are coming, he or she will often wait until a group is assembled before opening. It is pointless to get upset over these delays, since there is nothing you can do about it. Folks in a hurry should do their traveling offshore.

AVOIDING COLLISIONS

I don't know who said it first, or when, but it remains true today: a collision at sea can ruin your whole day. Whether it is life-threatening or just embarrassing, hitting someone (or something) should be avoided at all costs. It is the primary focus of the rules of the road.

One of the first, and most important, rules is: "Every vessel shall at all times maintain a proper lookout by sight and hearing as well as by all available means appropriate in the prevailing circumstances and conditions so as to make a full appraisal of the situation and of the risk of collision." Although few cruising boats, other than long-distance passagemakers, set formal watches, someone must be on watch—on deck, acting as lookout—anytime the boat is underway. Autopilots, radar, and other electronics are no substitute, especially in reduced visibility, for a human pair of eyes and ears.

To determine if you are on a collision course with another boat, take compass bearings on the boat. If the bearing does not change, your chances of collision are high. You can sight across the ship's compass, or use a hand-bearing compass. Never assume that just because you have the right-of-way the other boat will change course or speed. He might, but then again he might not. It's better for you to slow down, or make a course change early on, than to insist on your "rights" and ruin your whole day.

One of the hardest things to do is judge the speed of a large ship. A 300-foot container ship can be plowing along at nine or ten knots and give the appearance that it is standing still. Never argue with a ship, never get in their way, and never try to cross their bow, or cross too close to their stern where the prop wash creates dangerous turbulence. It can take a quarter-mile or more for a ship to come to a full stop, and your boat can be toothpicks before the ship has ground to a halt.

Towing

Sooner or later most of us offer another boat assistance in the form of a tow, or may need a tow ourselves. It's often to give a pull to someone who has run aground, or run out of fuel, or had an engine quit.

Towing can be dangerous business, and should be approached with care. A towline is under tremendous strain, and it can be a lethal weapon if it parts. Make sure no one is ever standing too close to, or in line with, the towline while it is under strain.

Nylon is the best for towing, since it will stretch and act as a shock absorber. However, if it parts it will snap back with enormous force. Braided nylon has less of a tendency to do this than three-strand, so it is the better choice.

Towing too fast is always asking for trouble, and commercial craft, including the Coast Guard, seem to be particularly bad about this. It's a great way to destroy fittings or cause the towline to part. And when you first start off, go very slowly, placing a gradual strain on the line.

Don't offer to tow another boat unless you are sure you can do so safely—when weather conditions are acceptable, when your boat and her gear are strong enough to handle the job, and when you feel confident about being able to maneuver without getting into trouble yourself. If you don't feel comfortable about doing it, offer to call for help if they haven't already, and to stand by until help arrives.

Be very careful if you accept a tow from another boat. Salvage laws are quite complicated, and more than one person has lost their boat because of salvage rights. A towboat is entitled to compensation for the work. Agree on a price up-front, and get it in writing if possible. If a claim should arise, you'll be in a better position if you were towed with your own line and not that of the towing boat.

GOING AGROUND

When we lived and cruised in Southern California, going aground was something we rarely thought about. Then we moved east, and soon learned that groundings, like no-see-ums, were pretty much a fact of life if you were going to spend much time at all cruising. Luckily, going aground is more often a frustration or an embarrassment than any kind of danger. Cruisers with twin-screw boats undoubtedly have the most to worry about if they run aground, since both rudders and props are out there in a position to be easily damaged.

If you have just touched bottom, the first reaction may be to jam the boat in reverse and try to back off quickly. This may work, or it may be asking for trouble, since you will be running the risk of sucking dirt or sand through the engine intake. I have also seen people try to power ahead and plow their way through a sand bar or mud bank. Again, this may work or it may drive the boat harder aground.

The best thing you can do, and do it as fast as possible, is to get an anchor set in deeper water. Use the dinghy to row out the anchor, and to take soundings all around the boat to determine the direction of deepest water. If you don't have a lead line to take soundings, you can use a fishing weight tied to a piece of string, or just pole yourself around with the boat hook. The anchor will hold the boat in position and keep her from going farther aground, and you may be able to use it to kedge off.

Before you start hauling on a kedge, consider the state of the tide. On a rising tide, it may be easier to just wait a bit and see if she will float off on her own. On a falling tide, you will either have to work very fast or accept the fact that you will be stuck for several hours.

If another boat comes to assist, a slow, steady pull will be the most helpful. Keep a strain on the anchor line, and just the wake from another boat may be enough to rock her free.

And if you do find yourself high and dry for some time while you wait for the tide or for help to arrive, you might as well take advantage of the situation—scrub the bottom, check the zincs and through-hulls, pretend you meant to do this all along.

EMERGENCIES

Emergencies can—and do—arise, and one of the most interesting things about them is that most of them could have been prevented. You know as well as I do that it's true. How many times have you put off doing some little maintenance chore because it was too messy, or too much trouble, only to have that little problem develop into a major one, and always at the worst possible moment? It's human nature to put off unpleasant tasks for as long as possible, even though we may pay dearly for it later.

Once an emergency does occur, handling it in a seamanlike manner means staying calm, thinking through the problem, and solving it in a logical, reasonable manner. Panic, yelling and shouting, and casting blame are all actions that have no place on a proper cruising boat.

I still remember being part of a delivery crew off the coast of California when we lost steerage on a dark, cold, windy night (emergencies never seem to happen in warm sunshine). The boat headed up into the wind and wallowed in the swells. The new owner, a man with little boating experience, panicked. He was yelling at all of us to "do something," he was blaming everyone for not checking the steering before we left, and demanding that someone call the Coast Guard at once for a tow. Luckily, the delivery captain remained calm. He pointed out that while the boat was uncomfortable in the seas, we were in deep water and in no immediate danger. The captain's first priority was to make a cup of coffee, and then assess the situation. It was the correct approach. The rudder quadrant, a Taiwanese casting, had broken, but the boat was equipped with an emergency tiller. In less than fifteen minutes we had the tiller installed and were underway again. The biggest loss, from the crew's viewpoint, was that we could no longer use the autopilot and had to steer by hand.

While some emergencies—manoverboard, a medical problem, etc.—demand immediate action, the majority, in fact, do not. Generally, it is best if you stop for a moment, catch your breath, and take the time to think through the problem. Unless you are in very deep water, dropping an anchor is frequently the right first step. If the boat is secure, you can devote your full attention to the crisis at hand.

Where you are will make a big difference in whether you have a real emergency or just an inconvenience. Going offshore, even just along the coast between harbors, and going to foreign countries, requires a greater degree of preparedness than cruising along inland rivers or waterways.

Inshore, help is likely to be as close as the nearest marina or boat yard, where you can find what you need or at least get to a telephone to track down parts or repair people. Still, being prepared is the best policy. Carrying spare parts, repair manuals and the right tools can mean the difference between an efficient job you do yourself (inshore or offshore), or calling for a tow or waiting dockside for days or weeks for the right part, or the right expert, to arrive.

The more self-sufficient you become, the better you will be able to deal with emergencies. Learning how to do your own work, and performing maintenance on a regular basis, will make it easier to troubleshoot problems when they do arise, or to spot potential problems before they become critical.

Medical emergencies can be the scariest. Most cruising people are in good health, or at least know of their own medical problems and carry a good supply of any medication they may require. But accidents can happen, even to the most careful.

Anyone setting out on a cruise owes it to themselves, and to the rest of the crew, to have at least a basic knowledge of first aid. If you don't know much more than where the aspirin bottle is located, I would recommend enrolling in a first-aid course, and a course in CPR (cardiopulmonary resuscitation).

There are quite a few first-aid kits on the market, some of them quite expensive—costing as much as $200. You will be better off, and probably spend half the money, if you make up your own. Catalogues that sell first-aid kits list the contents, which can be a starting point; you'll find you already have a lot of what's included. Your physician can help round out the list with suggestions and probably with prescriptions for antibiotics or other medications that aren't available over-the-counter. How extensive the kit should be will depend on where you plan to cruise, how long you will be away from civilization (if at all), and simply what makes you feel comfortable.

You can also join a service, such as MMAS (Marine Medical Advisory Service), that maintains a 24-hour hot line. A medical history is kept on file, and members can call the hot line via their VHF radio and receive advice from a physician. BOAT/U.S. members can join MMAS for $6.00 a year.

Whether you are dealing with a medical emergency, repairing a broken engine, or crossing paths with a tanker, seamanship encompasses knowing what to do, when to do it, and how to do it. It begins before you leave on a cruise, with making sure both you and the boat are prepared, and continues every day as you gain in experience and knowledge. This doesn't mean that the learning process is dull and dry. On the contrary, the more you know the more enjoyable it becomes. And certainly feeling calm and confident is a lot more fun than the heart-stopping panic of not knowing what to do next. Cruising is an endless learning experience, and it just gets better as you go along.

CHAPTER 11

Weather and Safety

IF THERE'S ONE topic of conversation that comes up the most often among cruising people, it has to be the weather. More than anything else, it's the weather that determines if and when we leave port, whether a passage will be safe and fun or dangerous and miserable, whether we choose to anchor in a roadstead or seek shelter at a dock. The weather influences what we wear, where we go, when we go, how we spend our time.

WEATHER FORECASTS

There are a number of different sources for marine weather. A good one—if you have a TV set aboard—is often the weather on a local television station. Besides just hearing the local forecast, you will be able to see the latest weather maps and satellite pictures, and get a good idea of developing fronts and long-range trends.

You can also receive weather maps by installing a weather facsimile recorder aboard (see the chapter on Navigation). In many ways this is better than a TV channel, because you will receive hard copy that can be studied at length, rather than a quick picture flashing on the screen (Figure 11-1). And the information is readily available; with TV, you may be in a fringe area and unable to tune in a local station.

Weather information is broadcast on both VHF and SSB radio channels. NOAA weather can be tuned in 24 hours a day on VHF. These are local forecasts, covering a specified area of inshore, coastal, and offshore waters (offshore only to a certain distance, usually the 1000-fathom line). You'll find as you travel along the coast that one station will fade into another one, and you will be switching between WX1, WX2, and WX3.

Besides carrying the weatherfax frequencies, weather broadcasts

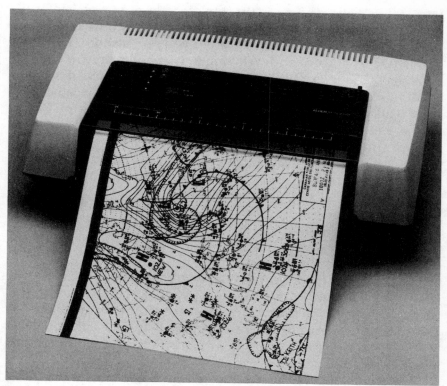

FIGURE 11−1. *A weather facsimile recorder, like this Marinefax TR-IV, can provide continuously updated weather information.* (*Courtesy Alden Electronics*)

are issued daily on SSB. These are not continuous like VHF, but are only given a few times a day at specified times. There is generally an offshore forecast once or twice a day, and a high-seas forecast once or twice a day.

Doing your own weather forecasting can be enjoyable, and if you are good at it, often more accurate than any weather forecast you might hear. This isn't because weather forecasters are bad at their jobs; it just means that much of our weather is quite local. You might look at the clouds and know that a violent thunderstorm is about to hit, while only a few miles away all is calm and serene. NOAA weather might be forecasting a high-percentage chance of squalls, but only you can look out a port and see what is happening in your immediate area.

To forecast with any accuracy, it is important to routinely enter your weather observations in the ship's log. Recording such information as barometric pressure, wind speed and direction, cloud formations and movements, and sea state if you are offshore, will make you aware of changes or developing trends, and help you interpret any forecasts you hear as they apply to your own particular position.

There are numerous books available about marine weather, and many colleges in coastal areas offer courses on weather forecasting for mariners. Taking a course, or just studying on your own, is one of the best things you can do in preparing for cruising. Weather is not as erratic as it sometimes seems; it does follow established patterns, and it is not all that difficult to learn enough to be able to make intelligent decisions about piloting and navigation.

FOG

At different times of the year, fog can be a persistent problem in some of the popular cruising grounds. Generally, fog occurs when warm, moist air flows over cold water. An exception is "sea smoke" or "steam fog," which happens when the air is cold and the water warm. It's a common occurrence on crisp autumn mornings, and usually dissipates rapidly as the air temperature warms.

Fog banks along the coast, however, can sometimes last for days. On one winter's trip south to Florida, I can remember spending a day and a night enveloped in fog off the coast of Georgia. We rejoined the

ICW at Fernandina Beach in Florida and found clear blue skies. For the next several days, we traveled in sunshine and could observe the fog bank as a solid wall just offshore across the barrier beaches.

I've always enjoyed the rather eerie quietude of fog—as long as the boat is securely anchored. Underway, the chances of going aground, hitting something, or being hit, are all too real, and extreme vigilance is necessary. We talked about fog in the chapter on navigation, but it bears further discussion.

Underway, you must signal by giving one long blast on the horn at least every two minutes. At anchor you are required to ring the ship's bell rapidly for about five seconds, at least every minute. An exception to this is that boats less than 20 meters (65.7 feet) anchored in a designated anchorage area do not have to signal.

Other boats are supposed to signal, too, of course, but unfortunately many of them don't. That's why it is so important both to slow down as much as possible, and to post a lookout forward. I know a few folks who never bother to signal until they hear another boat—then they will answer that boat's signal. It's a pretty silly, and dangerous, attitude when you think about it.

THUNDERSTORMS

Thunderstorms are a frequent occurrence along the East Coast of the United States during the summer, and a rarity on the West Coast where the cold water prevents their formation. Watching the approach of a thunderstorm, with its mass of dark, rolling clouds welling up to form a classic anvil-shape towering above the water, is an awe-inspiring sight.

About the only good thing you can say about thunderstorms is that they don't last very long—usually less than an hour. But while they may be short, they can be extremely dangerous, bringing hurricane-force winds, torrential rain, lightning and hail, as well as sometimes spawning tornadoes or waterspouts. Tornadoes almost always appear over land, but they have, on occasion, been known to move over a nearby water mass. Waterspouts are much weaker than tornados, and usually last only a few minutes to a half hour at the most. Although they are dangerous and you wouldn't want to motor into one, it is generally an easy matter to avoid them.

Since you have no way of knowing the strength of the wind in a thundersquall before it hits, it's a good idea to take down awnings, biminis, flags, anything that can be destroyed or blown away by high winds, at the first threat of a storm. Tie down any gear left on deck, or take it below if possible.

Being struck by lightning is one of the greatest fears of anyone out on the water during a thunderstorm. In the chapter on electricity, we talked about a grounding system for the boat, but there are other precautions you can take to protect yourself and your crew as well as the boat.

Try not to go on deck during the storm unless it is absolutely necessary. If you have gotten caught just before reaching a dock or the anchorage, then you will have to be topside to handle the lines or the anchor. Otherwise, stay in the cabin or belowdecks. And it should go without saying that no one should be in the water, whether swimming or diving, during a lightning storm.

If you must be on deck, don't touch anything metal—rails, cleats, rigging, stanchions, a radar mast—everything metal should be avoided. Whether topside or below, don't touch any object that is connected to the lightning ground system. And you definitely don't want to touch *two* such items so that you form a "bridge" between them, creating a perfect path for lightning to travel.

It's not a bad idea to disconnect any piece of electronics or other electrical gear, such as the TV or a computer, unless it must be in use for navigation purposes during the storm. Lightning strikes are rare, but they do happen; and a thunderstorm, no matter how common, is not to be taken lightly. A few common sense precautions should keep you, the crew, and the boat safe and in one piece.

HURRICANES

Like thunderstorms, hurricanes are more likely along the East and Gulf coasts than the West Coast of the United States—again because of the difference in water temperatures. Although hurricane season begins at the start of summer, the most frequent occurrences are in August and September, with quite a few in October as well.

The great debate among cruising people when a hurricane threatens is whether to stay aboard or get off the boat and go ashore.

The reasoning for staying aboard is that you will be there to "do something" in an emergency—reset anchors, fend off other boats, retie lines if you are at a dock. *Maybe* you could, in a minimal hurricane, with winds of "only" 65 to 70 knots. In 100 knots or more, you would not be able to stand up if you went out on deck, and all your strength would be used just for hanging on, not for performing any kind of work. With the amount of moisture in the air, it would be almost impossible to breathe, and your likelihood of drowning would be high.

About the only thing you can do, if you stay aboard at anchor, is to keep the engine running and power ahead slightly to try to relieve some of the strain on the anchor rodes. The problem with doing this is that you run the risk of damaging the prop from all the debris in the water—and there will be plenty in any harbor during a hurricane.

Whether to be dockside or at anchor is another decision to make, although there shouldn't be any question with this one. The worst possible place for a boat during a hurricane is tied to a dock. In fact, many marinas will not allow boats to remain at their docks during a storm, and with good reason. Docks are just not strong enough to withstand the strains imposed by the combination of wind, waves, storm tides, and heavy boats. When one dock goes, or one boat breaks loose, unbelievable damage can happen to the rest. Even though you may have done a seamanlike job of securing your boat, you still have no control over the rest of the marina crowd.

The rest of the crowd, of course, will also be your biggest problem at anchor. Harbors that are known as "hurricane holes" fill up fast when a storm threatens, and everyone naturally wants to set out several anchors, and as much scope as they possibly can. While that is exactly what they should do, it can create tight quarters in a hurry. In such conditions, it only takes one boat dragging anchor to wipe out the fleet.

There is little you can do to defend against bashing by other boats, other than to put out plenty of fenders. Lightweight yacht-type fenders are not likely to hold up. The big, round, vinyl ones like the commercial fishermen use are excellent. Old tires lashed all around the topsides will work even better.

Even though there is not always a lot of choice, try to pick a spot to anchor that will give the boat a relatively clear path if it does drag. It is better to go ashore in a marsh than against a cement wall or into somebody's weekend condo. Sometimes it is possible to run bow lines ashore to secure to trees or pilings and set the anchors off the stern. In some parts of Florida, people run their boats ashore in a mangrove swamp, which is a very secure way to ride out a storm.

If you do decide to leave the boat dockside, double-up on all the lines, and wrap plenty of chafe material around them at any potential wear spots. Chafe material could be lengths of garden hose, vinyl tubing, leather, or just old rags wrapped and tied around the line. (Anchor lines should receive chafe protection as well.) The boat should be well-fendered, and try to run lines to trees ashore if possible. A very real danger is that a storm tide will carry the boat higher than the dock's pilings and the boat will be impaled on a piling when the tide recedes. Set out stern anchors (bow anchors if you are tied stern-to), or breast anchors if you are side-tied, to try to hold the boat away from the dock.

Whether the boat is at a dock or anchored, remove absolutely everything topside that you can. You may lower and tie down a bimini during a thunderstorm, but for a hurricane the bimini and its framework should be removed and stowed below, along with all other canvas work. Ventilators should be removed and their flush-fitting deck plates inserted in the openings. An inflatable should be deflated and brought below, along with anything else small enough to fit through a hatch. A hard dinghy will have to be lashed securely, unless you are going ashore, in which case the dinghy can be carried to high ground and tied to a tree. If a dinghy is normally carried on davits, it is not a good idea to leave it there during a hurricane. Haul it aboard and lash it upside down on the foredeck or wherever it wants to go.

No matter how much you prepare, a hurricane will still do whatever it wants to. It is important to remember that gear can be replaced, but you and your crew are irreplaceable. Risking your life to save an inanimate object is foolhardy at best, deadly at worst. Do the best you can to get ready, then go below or go ashore and ride it out.

SAFETY ABOARD

I have finally come to the conclusion that safety is something writers like to write about, lecturers like to talk about, the Coast Guard likes to pass regulations about, and the average boat owner rarely, if ever, thinks about. Now really, how often do you go aboard your boat and immediately put on a life jacket? Do you even know where the life jackets are stowed? Does your crew?

But safety is important, so I'm going to write about it, even though I seldom think about it when we're cruising. The trick is to think about safety before leaving, equip the boat properly, run through a few drills with the crew so everyone feels comfortable about "what to do" in an emergency, and then you won't have to worry about it because everyone aboard will be prepared.

Safety in Bad Weather

While the best place to be during a storm is safely in port, sooner or later we all get caught out in bad weather. We may know that a cold front is approaching and mistakenly think we can reach the next harbor before it hits; or a lengthy offshore passage along the coast may start off in gentle morning breezes and deteriorate into a gale before nightfall.

Running for safe harbor may not always be the best choice—it's often a matter of timing. Many inlets along both coasts are "fair-weather" entrances; only a few are considered safe in all conditions. For instance, Absecon Inlet (Atlantic City, New Jersey) is an all-weather inlet, yet I remember coming in there once during a bad storm and it took a herculean effort on the helm to keep the boat from broaching. We made it in just fine, but I did wonder what conditions were like at the unacceptable inlets.

Even safe inlets can be extremely rough. Keep in mind that as seas build they will always be steeper and rougher where the water begins to shoal near shore; and if there is tide running against the wind, conditions will be even worse. The safest, but least comfortable, course may be to stay offshore and wait for things to calm down.

Frankly I have always felt better in a sailboat than a powerboat in really bad weather. A sailboat, with its ballasted hull, has a positive righting moment; and a cruising sailor can usually run off before a storm under shortened sail or heave-to and ride it out. While a true offshore cruising powerboat will be ballasted, most modern powerboats are not, especially the ones with semi-displacement or planing hulls. In addition, the high superstructure of flying bridges or double-decker cabins presents a lot of windage and an invitation to capsize.

In these conditions, it is extremely important that your engines be in top running condition, because their power is your safety. Depending on how your particular boat handles, it may be better to run off before a storm, putting her stern to wind and waves; or if they are too great (generally in winds over 25 or 30 knots), you may have to take the seas head-on. Under no circumstances do you want to let a powerboat present her beam to strong winds and big waves.

Until the weather calms, no one, including you, should be allowed out on deck unless they are wearing both a life jacket and a harness with a tether that can be clipped to a strong attachment point. The last thing you need to worry about in bad weather is someone going over the side.

Equipping the Boat

While the Coast Guard requires that all boats carry certain safety items—approved life jackets, flares, fire extinguishers, etc.—a well-found cruising boat needs additional gear.

Lifelines and Stanchions

Lifelines and stanchions are a good safety feature, as long as they are the correct height—30 to 36 inches. Too often they are only around 24 inches, which is just right to catch someone across the back of their knees and flip them over the side. Stanchions should be installed with through bolts and sturdy backing plates; otherwise, they won't be able to withstand the weight of a person falling against them.

Handholds

Handrails should also be through-bolted, not just screwed in place. You should be able to move anywhere on the boat and have something to grab ahold of. Handrails are for the safety of the crew—using them as a place to stow gear (boat hooks, dinghy oars, etc.) defeats their purpose. Install padeyes on the cabin top to use as hold downs for lashing gear, and leave the handrails free and unobstructed.

Handrails are also necessary belowdecks. Powerboats can roll and pitch in a seaway, and getting thrown across the wide expanse of a full-width cabin is not a pleasant experience. If the boat doesn't have plenty of handrails, think about installing them on the underside of the cabin top, next to ladders, along the carlines, in the engine room, in the galley, and in the heads.

Radar Reflectors

One piece of safety gear seldom seen on a powerboat is a radar reflector, probably because most powerboats carry radar itself. Yet a reflector is still a good idea—if you are anchored in fog, for example, or underway and your radar is on the blink. The only caution with installing a radar reflector is not to put it too close to your radar's antenna. Check your radar installation manual before installing the reflector.

Although there are numerous new and expensive radar reflectors on the market, one of the best is still the inexpensive ($40 to $60) octahedral cluster type, such as the Echomaster reflector made by Davis Instruments mounted correctly in the "catch rain" position.

Life Rafts

Unless your cruising is limited strictly to protected waterways in the warm latitudes, you need to think about carrying a life raft. To many, it is a huge expense ($2,000 to $5,000) for something that is—hopefully—just going to sit there. But if you should need it, there is no substitute and the price is cheap if it saves your life, or the lives of your loved ones.

A life raft, with its canopy enclosure and double bottom, offers much greater protection from exposure to the elements than the open boat used as the ship's tender, as well as reducing the risk of hypothermia (lowering of the body temperature that leads eventually to death).

There are cruisers who feel that the ship's tender is adequate, claiming they feel better knowing they can sail, row or use the outboard to get themselves closer to shore or closer to rescue. Which school of thought you subscribe to will depend primarily on where you plan to cruise, but if being prepared is the key to peace of mind and relaxed cruising, then make the investment in safety and get a life raft.

An abandon-ship kit can be kept near the life raft. It can include a jug of drinking water, dye markers and flares, a whistle, a signal mirror, an EPIRB (Emergency Position Indicating Radio Beacon) (Figure 11-2), a hand-bearing compass, a knife, emergency food rations, and a first-aid kit. If you will be making long hauls along the coast, you could also include fishing gear, a solar still for fresh water, and a radar reflector. This all sounds like a lot of gear, but actually it will stow in a canvas duffle that takes up little stowage space.

Life Jackets

A life jacket contributes nothing toward safety unless it is worn, and we all know how often that happens. A large part of the reason they are seldom put on, even in bad weather, is that they are bulky and uncomfortable. There are inflatable vests available that are comfortable to wear since they are flat unless you inflate them. They are not "approved," but if they are something you would actually put on then they are worth having.

At least keep the life jackets in a place where they are easy to grab in an emergency, and make sure everyone aboard knows where that place is. It's a good idea to attach a plastic whistle and a small personal strobe or light stick to each life jacket.

Safety Harnesses

Anytime someone goes on deck in bad weather, or at night (even on a calm night), they should be wearing a harness with a tether that can be attached to the boat. Lifelines are not always strong enough to be a good attachment point, but handholds are generally excellent for this purpose.

A harness and tether should also be used if you must go over the side in rough water to free a fouled prop or check for some other damage.

Manoverboard

Probably the biggest fear of anyone going out on the water is losing someone overboard. True, we don't think much about it on a weekend trip in home territory; but anyone heading offshore, even briefly, and anyone cruising shorthanded, should think about it a lot.

Manoverboard gear should be mounted close to the helm, where it

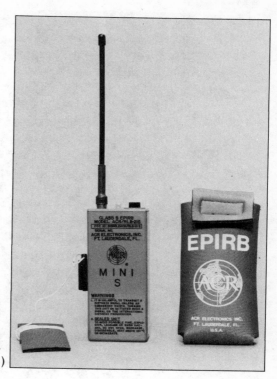

FIGURE 11–2. *An "S" class EPIRB is designed specifically to attach to a life raft, like this RLB 21S from ACR Electronics. (Courtesy ACR Electronics, Inc.)*

can be grabbed and tossed over the side instantly. A manoverboard system typically will include a life-ring with a whistle, a dye marker, and a small sea anchor (a drogue) attached to it. A floating strobe light is attached to the life ring with about five feet of polypropylene line, and a man-overboard pole is attached with another 25 feet of polypropylene. This arrangement is seen more often on sailboats than on powerboats. But don't be fooled; people can fall overboard on powerboats as easily as they can on sailboats.

If all the gear is hard to stow near the helm on a powerboat—and it frequently is—a good alternative is the SEAID and heaving line from Survival Technologies in St. Petersburg, Florida (Figure 11-3). The SEAID automatically inflates to a horseshoe with 25 pounds of buoyancy within two to four seconds after hitting the water. The heaving line includes 75 feet of floating line and a grab loop and buoyancy ball for the person in the water to hang on to. Together, the two items cost under $150 and can be mounted just about anywhere.

FIGURE 11–3. *The SEAID and heaving line are an excellent manoverboard system that can be mounted just about anywhere.* (*Courtesy Survival Technologies Group*)

Before leaving on a cruise, you owe it to yourself and your crew to go out and practice manoverboard maneuvers. It's the only way for everyone to develop confidence in their ability to handle the boat, and to figure out the best way to get someone back aboard. On most powerboats, backing down to get someone aboard via a ladder from the swim step is generally the easiest way. When you get close to someone in the water, put the engines in neutral to avoid sucking them into the props.

The best approach, of course, is prevention. Don't go overboard in the first place. That's why it is so important to hold on, and to wear at least a harness (preferably a harness and a life jacket) so if you do slip you don't leave the boat—and the boat doesn't leave you.

Both weather and safety will play a big part in any cruise. Weather we will think about a lot, safety we will think about only in an emergency. But the key to dealing with both is preparedness. Understanding the weather will help us forecast it as well as know how to prepare for what it will bring. And we will only have a safe cruise if we prepare for it before we ever leave—by equipping the boat, and ourselves, so that staying safe, doing things in a safe and seamanlike manner, are simply second nature to us.

CHAPTER 12

Getting Ready

BUYING THE BOAT may have seemed like a major undertaking, but it pales when compared to the work, and the fun, of getting ready to take off for a cruise. All the planning and preparation, the making of lists, the shopping and stowage, the attending to endless details, are tasks that I personally enjoy. But if such organization is not your cup of tea, then try to find someone in the crew who *will* think of it as fun instead of work, and you'll get the docklines untied a lot sooner.

PLANNING THE CRUISE

I know a few (very few) folks who can throw some supplies aboard and take off for months with seemingly no effort. Most of us, however, require a certain amount of time, after making the "let's go cruising" decision, to set everything in motion. It's been my experience that the more effort I put into the planning stages, the more I enjoy the cruise.

You might think that a lot of planning would have the opposite effect, that it would remove the spontaneity and therefore much of the joy. But I've found that adequate planning and preparation adds to our spontaneity as well as to our sense of freedom. If we find ourselves in a lovely, remote anchorage and decide to stay a week instead of a day as planned, we have the freedom to do so because the boat is prepared. We have plenty of food, water and fuel, books to read, all equipment is in working order and there are spares if anything does break. Let's consider some of the things to think about in the planning stages.

Charts

Although charts are a necessity, they can also be a major expense if you are planning an extended cruise. One way to cut down on the cost, and get some extras to boot, is to purchase chart kits.

We prefer the BBA chart kits because they are accurate reproductions of NOS charts and are printed in full color, and using the same colors as the original charts. The biggest advantage to the kits is that they contain large-scale charts of virtually every harbor in each particular area—no matter how small the harbor. If you were to purchase each chart separately you would spend several hundred dollars more than the cost of the kit. The BBA chart kits run from $45 for the small-format kits up to $100 for a large-format kit of the Bahamas.

What generally happens if you purchase each one separately is that you pick and choose, deciding in advance exactly where you are going to go. Now *that* removes the spontaneity. An all-inclusive chart kit gives you the option of making choices as you go along.

Most of the BBA chart kits include aerial photographs of a number of harbors. These are invaluable when making landfall in an unfamiliar area, or approaching a harbor entrance for the first time.

The only disadvantage we have found with the kits is that we have difficulty plotting the days run if it spans several pages. For that reason, we purchase small scale charts that cover as wide an area as possible to use as an overall chart, and rely on the kits for close-in and harbor piloting. This combination has proven to be an excellent one.

Charts, of course, are limited to just the water and a small amount of the land adjacent to it. In addition to charts, we like to carry road maps to get a better feel for the surrounding countryside. It gives us an idea of what towns are nearby, even though inland, and what points of interest we might like to visit (either by renting a car, or taking public transportation if it's available).

Cruising Guides

Considering the number of cruising guides available, I sometimes wonder if there is anyplace left on earth that has not had a guide written about it. Most of them are very informative and can be an indispensable reference as you travel along, besides providing enjoyable reading on a cold winter's night when next summer's cruise is still a dream. You'll find hard-cover books, like Marjorie Cahn Brazer's excellent *Cruising Guide to the Great Lakes* or Duncan and Ware's *Cruising Guide to the New England Coast,* to name just two, that include much of the author's own experiences and expertise; as well as softcover guides that are more "technical" and that are updated yearly, like the *Waterway Guide*'s regional editions that include current listings of marinas and other available services.

But don't limit yourself to just cruising guides. I like to learn as much as I can about an area before we get there, and find that "land" guides, such as Fodor's and others, often give more of the history and general ambiance of a place than the guides written specifically for boats. And they usually have a better listing of restaurants and shops than the marine guides.

Writing to the chamber of commerce or tourist bureaus in towns along the way can bring a wealth of information about an area. For just one example, I recently wrote to the Department of Transportation for the state of New York, and received a package that included charts, maps, a newsletter, and several brochures containing a tremendous amount of detail about New York's canals and waterways—depths, clearances, methods of operation—all of which is valuable information for the planning of our next cruise to the Great Lakes via the canal system.

Passports

Passports, and sometimes visas, are often required if you are leaving the country. But it is a good idea to have a passport even if you are only cruising in the United States. It is the best form of identification you can carry. Whether you are having money transferred, cashing a check, or completing any type of transaction that requires identification, you'll find that a passport is accepted much more readily than any other form, including a driver's license (particularly an out-of-state driver's license).

We have found that most transactions, from cashing checks to receiving mail, are invariably easier to accomplish in a small town than a city. As a rule, people are just friendlier, more trusting, and easier to deal with away from metropolitan areas.

Reservations

This definitely removes the spontaneity, but if you are going to a popular resort area during the "high season," and are planning on going dockside, you undoubtedly will need to make reservations well in advance.

We once made reservations at a marina in Nassau three months in advance, and I know of several marinas in New England that require advance notice of almost that long. If you have any doubts at all, it's best to call as soon as you think about it, and find out what is required. Some places get so crowded on summer weekends that it is difficult to find a spot to anchor, let alone find an empty slip. We personally prefer to avoid these areas if at all possible, but if you or your crew insist, then calling ahead is a must.

Many resort areas are only overwhelmed on weekends, and will have plenty of accommodations during the week. This is the best way to go, and you're more likely to find space at the marina, fewer crowds in restaurants and shops, and the locals friendlier.

Mail Delivery

Receiving mail is always high on everyone's priority list. It seems like the longer we are away, and the farther we go, the more important it becomes.

It is vital to choose someone who is absolutely reliable to handle the forwarding of your mail. For many, this is a family member; others use their office staff, their banker or broker, or a secretarial service. We have used a mail-forwarding service, MCCA Inc., in Estes Park, Colorado, for over ten years now.

MCCA receives and holds our mail and packages until they receive our instructions for shipping (they will also ship on a schedule if you prefer). They will ship by US mail, UPS, Federal Express—any way you want it; and they will receive and deliver telephone messages for members as well.

While there are a number of mail forwarding services around (check the classifieds in boating magazines), we like MCCA because they maintain a 24-hour 800 number, which can cut turnaround time in half. A service that requires you to mail them each new address, rather than telephone, or that you can call only during certain hours, can add several days to your waiting time. Also, after ten years, we can honestly say we have never had a single problem with MCCA's service—they are reliable, efficient, and pleasant to deal with. Their address is:

MCCA, Inc.
P.O. Box 2870
Estes Park, CO 80517
1-800-525-5304

Annual dues for MCCA are $150, plus a one-time registration fee of $15, and a postage deposit of $35.00. Postage is billed as the deposit runs low.

The only disadvantage with a mail forwarding service is that you must send out change-of-address notices to all your correspondents, which may be too much trouble unless you are heading out for an extended cruise (six months or longer). A family member would presumably go to your home or post office to pick up your mail.

Have all your mail forwarded by first class or "priority" mail, or use one of the fast services like Federal Express or UPS overnight or second-day air. Anything else, such as parcel post, can take too long. I have seen folks get hung up for a week, two weeks, or longer, waiting for mail or packages to arrive.

The address of any mail sent to you should include both your name and the name of the boat, and in a lower corner "Hold for Arrival." Most importantly, if your agent is sending more than one package or envelope, each one should be marked "1 of 2," "2 of 2," etc. Mail sent on the same day does not always arrive on the same day. You could easily think you have picked up your mail and leave for the next port, never knowing that more mail arrived a day or two later.

I have been successful with having mail sent c/o general delivery, although a friend of mine once waited for several weeks for a package, making daily trips to the post office. It was only after creating a scene and refusing to leave the window, while the line of customers behind him grew more irate by the minute, that the package was found—the clerk had misplaced it and couldn't be bothered to institute a search until he was threatened.

But most of the time, general delivery works well in the United States. Post offices will hold mail for ten to fifteen days—the time varies from town to town. Keep in mind, however, that not all post offices will accept general delivery mail; it is usually just the main post office in a town and not the branch offices. Some cruising guides, such as the *Waterway Guide*, will list not just mail drops but whether or not the post office is within walking distance of the harbor.

Other places to consider as mail drops include marinas, yacht clubs, hotels, banks, American Express offices, and the office of the Port Captain for the harbor. Just be sure to make all arrangements before telling your agent to ship the mail.

Money Matters

I remember, when I first started cruising, how difficult it was to cash a check anywhere but at my own bank. Trying to convince a teller I was who I said I was, regardless of the amount of identification I presented, was an exercise destined to make me feel like a criminal. All that has changed now that we have teller machines, which will accept a card and code number without making a fuss.

Most bank cards will work at branches of your own bank and with one or two, sometimes more, national systems. There are still enough different systems so it is not always easy to find one that you can use. My bank card will work with "Relay" and "Cirrus," and I have been able to find one or the other in most towns from North Carolina to Florida. On the other hand, a friend from New York recently tied up at our dock and we were unable to find a bank in this area that would accept his NYCE card. Charges for using the cards can range from $.25 to $1.50 for each transaction.

With a bank card, you can usually withdraw only $100 or $200 a day. For larger amounts of cash, it is easier to use an international credit card, like Visa or Mastercard, to get a cash advance at a member bank. Or just use the credit cards whenever you can so there is no need to carry large amounts of cash.

We carry some cash (seldom over $500) and $1,000 to $2,000 in traveler's checks. Traveler's checks cost 1 percent of the face value of the check, and are a bargain considering the safety they offer. If you carry traveler's checks, purchase them in small denominations—mostly twenties, and never anything greater than a fifty. It's just too difficult to cash checks for larger amounts in out-of-the-way places.

PREPARING FOR THE CRUISE

Planning a cruise can span many months; for some, even years. But the preparation will be compressed into weeks, and that's when the excitement really starts to build. When you see boxes of groceries and spare parts piling up on the dock, someone is hoisting the dinghy aboard, and someone else is tuning up the engine and checking out the electronics, then you know the time is drawing near when all those dreams and plans become reality and you are on your way at last. But don't untie the lines just yet.

Making Lists

Now is the time to make lists—for me, that means a spiral notebook because I make a lot of lists, and little pieces of paper are too easy to lose. But making lists is the only way you are going to remember what needs to be done, what needs to be purchased, and where it is all going to go.

Preparing the Boat

If you are like most boat owners, you already keep your boat in good running order. But if it's "almost" time for an oil change, or a tune-up, go ahead and do it before leaving for a cruise, while it is still an easy matter to drive to a local store for parts and you know your local mechanic is readily available if you need him. It won't be so simple once you are out in the boondocks, or just in an unfamiliar place.

Your engine and generator may be well-known and popular makes, so you would think parts and filters would be easy to find anywhere. Don't bet on it. That's what we thought when we started cruising, and discovered that everyone seemed to carry parts for every engine but ours. We now carry enough oil to last the cruise (it's usually cheaper by the case anyway), as well as spare oil and fuel filters, belts, diaphragms or impellers for the pumps—all the spares and tools, as well as the shop manual, that will allow us to perform routine maintenance or make repairs ourselves. How much you carry in the way of spares will depend on how long and where you are cruising, but the more you take along, the better.

The boat should be hauled for bottom-cleaning, and for the inspection of zincs, through-hulls, propellers, and other underwater fittings. Again, carrying spare zincs or spares for other fittings is not a bad idea (wooden plugs for all through-hulls should be carried as a safety measure). The one thing not to carry is spare bottom-paint. Just about every boat yard around requires that owners purchase bottom paint through the yard—regardless of whether the owner or the yard is doing the work—so having spare paint is just added weight.

All electronics and electrics should be thoroughly checked out, including the batteries. If they are old and tired, you might be better off to go ahead and replace them now and save yourself a lot of grief later on. And now is the time to think about spares for all those little things you never think about—like spare bulbs for both interior and exterior lights, extra batteries for flashlights and radios, spare wire, fuses or breakers, terminals, and a soldering iron.

Repair kits are important for all "essential" equipment, such as the heads, freshwater pumps, the galley stove. If your boat is not equipped with a manual backup pump for the fresh water, I would definitely carry a spare electric pump in addition to the repair kit.

Provisioning

How much stocking-up you do of non-perishable items (canned and packaged foods as well as paper towels, toilet tissue, etc.) will again depend on where you are going and how long you will be gone, but there are a few points to keep in mind.

Once you leave home you will seldom have a car at your disposal, and grocery stores are not always close to the harbor. Convenience stores and marinas (which sometimes carry a small selection of provisions) are very expensive places to shop compared to a large supermarket. Some marinas do have courtesy cars available, but it's not something you can count on.

Perhaps more importantly, you may not be able to find the brands you like. This may not matter on a lot of items, and certainly sampling new treats is part of the fun of cruising, but if there are certain things that you *are* very particular about, then be sure to carry enough to last the cruise. For instance, we are particular about our brand of coffee, so if we are leaving on a six-month cruise, I buy six large jars of Taster's Choice coffee and stash them aboard wherever I can find the room.

The same idea works in reverse. When we are in Florida, I always buy enough Key Lime juice to have plenty when we get back home, because we can't buy it at any of our local stores; and in the Bahamas, I buy cases of Pender's Ginger Beer to take home.

Even if you know you will be able to shop frequently, buy enough to carry at least one spare of personal items, like toothpaste and shampoo. And if you wear eyeglasses, carrying an extra pair is definitely a necessity if you cannot operate the boat without them. And get in touch with your physician and obtain an adequate supply of any prescription drugs or medications you require.

If you will be cruising and away from home during holidays or special family celebrations like birthdays or anniversaries, by all means take along enough goodies to make it a real celebration aboard ship. For example, for Christmas you might include a few favorite family decorations, or ornaments and a tiny imitation tree to hang them on. Take the family stockings and hang them up around the pilot house. Having your own personal treasures around will make it feel like a traditional holiday celebration, and they go a long way toward easing any homesick feelings that can crop up at special times of the year.

Stowage

I'm always amazed by how quickly things can get lost aboard a boat. There are, after all, only a certain number of lockers and bins, and you would think that it would be a simple matter to find a storage spot for something and then be able to retrieve it a month or two later. It never seems to happen that way, at least not for me (or for Taz).

In my "list notebook" I sketch out the accommodation plan of the boat, showing the location of every single stowage place, no matter how small, and assign each one a number. Then I give each locker at least a page, and list everything that it contains.

If I am really feeling organized, I list everything aboard in alphabetical order, then cross-reference each item to its locker. Mostly having the list just means that either of us, or any guests we have aboard, can "search" for something without having to empty entire lockers, many of which are packed tightly.

Away at Last

There's always a tug when we leave for a cruise. It isn't there for a weekend trip, but when I know we are leaving our wonderful little house-on-stilts, our friends, and our all-too-familiar surroundings for a couple of months or longer, there is definitely a feeling of sadness and a bit of trepidation—no matter how well we have prepared. For me, these feelings last until our dock is no longer in sight and the shoreline of Oriental is receding in our wake. Then pure excitement takes over, along with a feeling of well-being and the knowledge that we have once again escaped the work-a-day world and new sights and new adventures lie ahead . . . and I can't *wait* to experience them.

Obviously the better prepared you and the boat are, the more confident you are in both the boat and your own abilities, the easier the transition will be from shore to sea. Just don't get bogged down in too many details (and this is an easy thing to do, particularly if it is your first long cruise). There comes a point when enough is enough, and little things *can* be left until later.

You can read, you can study, you can take courses, you can spend money and more money, but the only way you actually go cruising is simply this: You go. Don't wait until you feel the boat is "perfect," or every last item is crossed off the list, or you may never leave. And once you do leave, you will discover the great appeal of cruising—it's fun! Cruising is worth all the effort that goes into the planning stages;

it is worth whatever you invested in time and money. Because once you are out there, making memories and experiencing the natural way of life aboard your own boat, you know you'll never regret having done it, and most likely you are going to do it over and over again. It's an experience that can easily become a way of life—and it's definitely one of the best.

List of Manufacturers

ONE OF MY PET peeves has always been to read about the virtues of a particular piece of gear, decide that I want it, and then be unable to find it, or even find out who makes it. So the following is a list of manufacturers that are mentioned in this book. It is not a list of every manufacturer of marine gear (there are plenty of catalogues around that do that), but it does give the address of everyone covered in the book, so hopefully if anything grabs your interest you will be able to locate the maker.

ACR Electronics, Inc.
P.O. Box 5247
Fort Lauderdale, FL 33310
305–981–3333

Alden Electronics
Washington Street
Westborough, MA 01581
617–366–8851

American Boat and Yacht Council, Inc.
(publishers of "Standards and Recommended Practices for Small Craft")
P.O. Box 747
Millersville, MD 21108
301-923–3932

American Ladder Corporation
2120 S.W. 58 Avenue
Hollywood, FL 33023
305–962–0077

Aquadrive Systems, Inc.
55 Olin Street
Ocean Grove, NJ 07756
201–502–0068

Atkins & Hoyle Limited
71 Portland Street
Toronto, Canada M5V 2M9
416–596–1818

Basic Designs, Inc.
5815 Bennett Valley Road
Santa Rosa, CA 95404
707–575–1220

Jay R. Benford
P.O. Box 447
RD 1, Box 127, Radcliffe Avenue
St. Michaels, MD 21663
301–745–3235

Bomar, Inc.
South West Street
P.O. Box W
Charlestown, NH 03603
603–826–5791

Boston Whaler
1149 Hingham St.
Rockland, MA 02370
617–871–1400

Canon USA
One Canon Plaza
Lake Success, NY 11042
516–488–6700

Caterpillar Inc.
Engine Division
P.O. Box 610
Mossville, IL 61552
309–578–8148

DaHon California, Inc.
2949 Whipple Road
Union City, CA 94587
415–471–6330

Daimen Corporation
449 N. Pennsylvania Ave.
Morrisville, PA 19067
215–736–1383

Datamarine International, Inc.
53 Portside Drive
Pocasset, MA 02559
508–563–7151

Davis Instruments
3465 Diablo Avenue
Hayward, CA 94545
415–732–9229

Down East Sails & Canvas
P.O. Box 363
Oriental, NC 28571
919–249–1004

Dytek Laboratories, Inc.
165 Keyland Court
Bohemia, NY 11716
516–589–9030

The Edson Corporation
460 Industrial Park Road
New Bedford, MA 02745
508-995-9711

Espar Heater Systems
6435 Kestrel Road
Mississauga, Ontario
Canada L5T 1Z8
416–670–0960

Fireboy Halon Systems Division
Convenience Marine Products, Inc.
P.O. Box 152
Grand Rapids, MI 49501
616–454–8337

Furuno USA Inc.
P.O. Box 2343
South San Francisco, CA 94083
415–873–4421

Galley Maid Marine Products, Inc.
4348 Westroads Drive
West Palm Beach, FL 33407
407–848–8696

The Guest Company, Inc.
P.O. Box 2059 Station A
Meriden, CT 06450
203–238–0550

Hatteras Yachts
Division of Genmar Industries, Inc.
2100 Kiroett Drive
P.O. Box 2690
High Point, NC 27261
919–889–6621

Heart Interface Corp.
811 1st Ave. S
Kent, WA 98032
206–859–0640

Hubbell Wiring Device Division
Hubbell Inc.
P.O. Box 3999
Bridgeport, CT 06605
203–337–3348

ICOM America, Inc.
2380—116th Ave. NE
Bellevue, WA 98004
206–454–8155

Imtra Corporation
30 Barnet Blvd.
New Bedford, MA 02745
508–990–2700

Instapure Water Filter
Teledyne Water Pik
1730 E. Prospect
Fort Collins, CO 80525
303–484–1352

Johannsen Boat Works
P.O. Box 570097
Miami, FL 33257
305–445–7534

Johnson Marine
C. Sherman Johnson Co., Inc.
P.O. Box L, Route 82, Industrial Park
East Haddam, CT 06423
203–873–8697

Kadey-Krogen Yachts, Inc.
1310 N.W. 18th Avenue
Miami, FL 33125
305–326–0266

Lands' End, Inc.
1 Lands' End Lane
Dodgeville, WI 53595
1–800–356–4444

Lightning Electronics Inc.
P.O. Box 1207
Cabot, AR 72023
501–843–6561

Magnavox
Marine and Survey Systems Division
2829 Maricopa Street
Torrance, CA 90503
213–618–1200

Marinco Electrical Products
One Digital Drive
Novato, CA 94949
415–883–3347

Martin Marine Company
Box 251—Goodwin Road
Kittery Point, Maine 03905
207–439–1507

Maxwell Marine, Inc.
629 Terminal Way, Suite 1
Costa Mesa, CA 92627
714–631–2634

Micrologic
20801 Dearborn Street
Chatsworth, CA 91311
818–998–1216

Minolta Corporation
101 Williams Drive
Ramsey, NJ 07446
201–825–4000

Mooring Products Corporation
1189 North U.S. Hwy. #1
Ormond Beach, FL 32074
1–800–277–9447

Mystic Color Lab
Mason's Island Road
P.O. Box 144
Mystic, CT 06355
1–800–367–6061

Nautical Engineering
P.O. Box 5380
Northville, MI 48167
313–349–7077

New England Ropes, Inc.
Popes Island
New Bedford, MA 02740
508–999–2351

Nicro Marine
2065 West Avenue 140th
San Leandro, CA 94577
415–357–8332

Nordic Tugs, Inc.
P.O. Box 1325
Woodinville, WA 98072
206–481–5502

Onan
1400 73rd Ave. N.E.
Minneapolis, MN 55432
612–574–5000

Oriental Sailmakers
P.O. Box 768
Oriental, NC 28571
919–249–2895

Peugeot
Cycles Peugeot USA, Inc.
555 Gotham Parkway
Carlstadt, NJ 07072
201–460–7000

Racor Division
Parker Hannifin Corporation
P.O. Box 3208
Modesto, CA 95353
800–344–3286

Raritan Engineering Company, Inc.
P.O. Box 1157
Millville, NJ 08332
609–825–4900

Ray Jefferson Company
Division of Jetronic Industries Inc.
Main & Cotton Sts.
Philadelphia, PA 19127
215–487–2800

Raytheon Marine Company
46 River Road
Hudson, NH 03051
603–881–5200

Rolls Battery Engineering
P.O. Box 671
Salem, MA 01970
508–745–3333

Sabre Yachts
Hawthorne Road, Box 10
South Casco, ME 04077
207–655–5050

Sea Recovery Corporation
P.O. Box 2560
Gardena, Ca 90247
213–327–4000

Seagull Water Purification Systems
General Ecology of New England
P.O. Box 271
Trumbull, CT 06611
203–384–9335

Shakespeare Company
Rt. 3, P.O. Box 733
Newberry, SC 29108
803–276–5504

Skowhegan Moccasin
P.O. Box 516
Lewiston, ME 04243
207–784–1362

So-Pac
South Pacific Associates, Ltd.
4918 Leary Ave. NW
Seattle, WA 98107
1–800–227–6722

Soundown Corporation
45 Congress Street, Suite 1
Salem, MA 01970
617–598–4248

Standard Communications Corporation
P.O. Box 92151
Los Angeles, CA 90009
213–532–5300

Surrette America
Division of Atlantic Battery Co., Inc.
P.O. Box 249
Tilton, NH 03276
603–286–7770

Survival Technologies Group
101 16th Avenue South
St. Petersburg, FL 33701
1–800–525–2747

Trace Engineering
5917–195th N.E.
Arlington, WA 98223
206–435–8826

Venture Marine Inc.
8403 Huron River Drive
Ypsilanti, MI 48197
313–482–6250

Webasto Heater, Inc.
1458 East Lincoln
Madison Hts., MI 48071
313–545–8770

Wolter Systems
1100 Harrison Avenue
Cincinnati, Ohio 45214
513–651–2666

Index